THE KREGEL PICTORIAL GUIDE TO CHRISTIAN HERITAGE IN ENGLAND

DANIEL A. SCALBERG

kregel
PUBLICATIONS

Grand Rapids, MI 49501

The Kregel Pictorial Guide to Christian Heritage in England

© 2002 by Daniel A. Scalberg

Published by Kregel Publications, a division of Kregel, Inc., P.O. Box 2607, Grand Rapids, MI 49501. Kregel Publications provides trusted, biblical publications for Christian growth and service. For more information about Kregel Publications, visit our web site: www.kregel.com.

Photo Acknowledgments:
The Lindisfarne Gospel (Beginning of St. Matthew's Gospel 1000325.011), *The British Library, London, England*

Bede, John Wesley, William Wilberforce, *The Jeffreys Archive, Golden, Colorado*

Elizabeth I with autograph, *North Wind Picture Archives, Alfred, Maine*

Thomas More, *Three's Company, London, England*

C. S. Lewis, Dorothy Sayers, *courtesy of the Marion E. Wade Center, Wheaton College, Wheaton, Illinois*

The author gratefully acknowledges the kind permission to publish photographs taken by the author from:

    The Abbey Office, Bath Abbey
    Curator, Winchester Cathedral
    The Dean and Chapter, Canterbury Cathedral
    The Dean and Chapter, Durham Cathedral
    The Dean and Chapter, Ely Cathedral
    The Dean and Chapter, St. Giles Cathedral
    The Dean and Chapter, St. Paul's Cathedral
    The Dean and Chapter, Salisbury Cathedral
    The Dean and Chapter, Wells Cathedral
    The Dean and Chapter, Westminster
    The Dean and Chapter, Winchester
    The Dean and Chapter, York

ISBN 0-8254-3663-x

Printed in Hong Kong

1 2 3 4 5 / 05 04 03 02 01

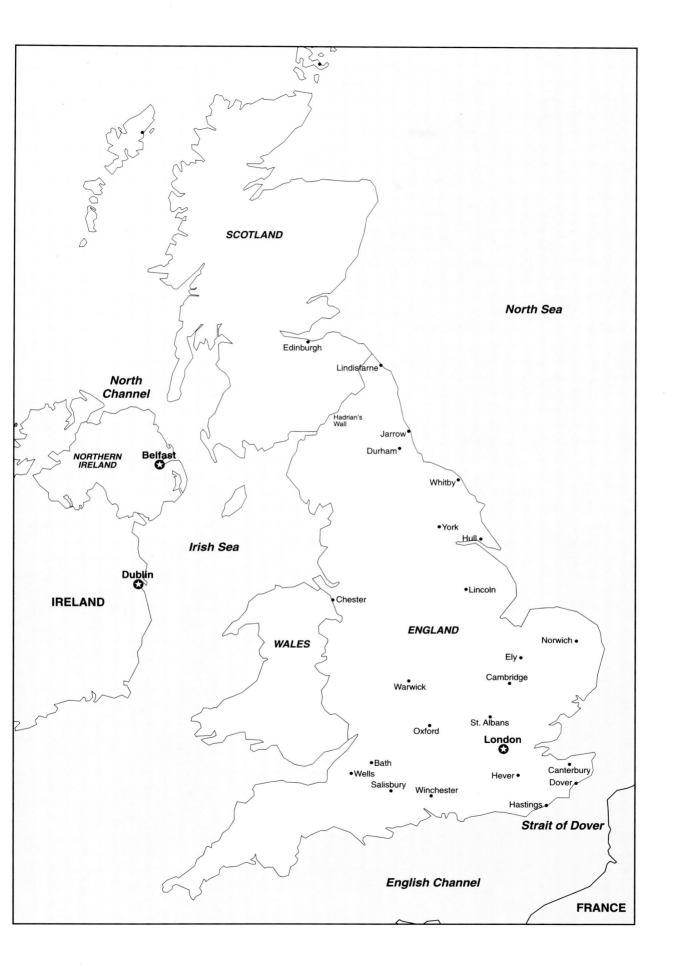

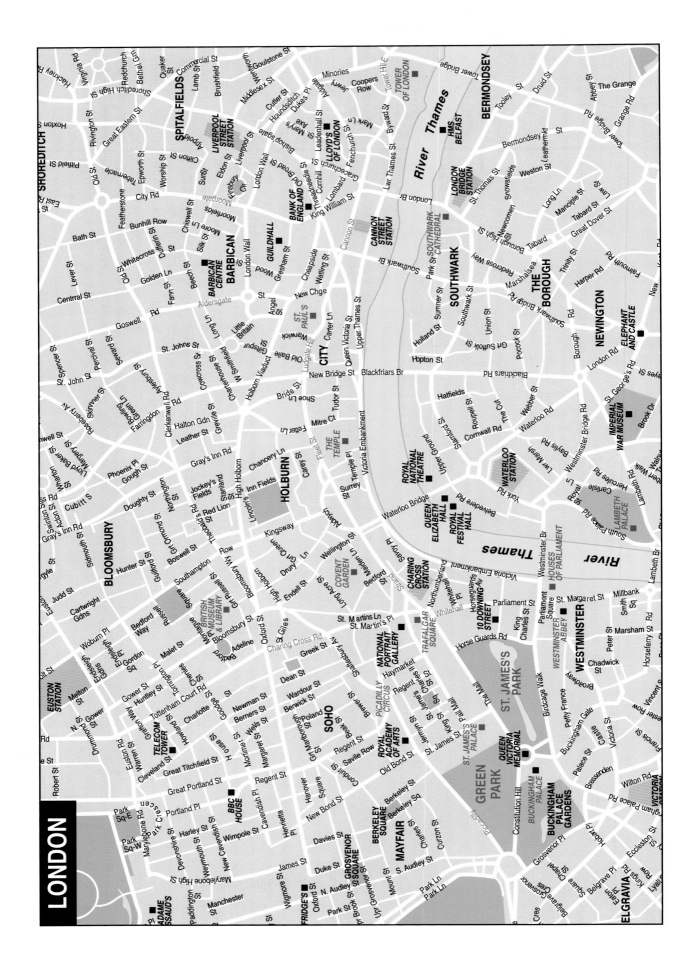

CONTENTS

PREFACE

Welcome to a stroll through English church history. Written for the Christian layperson with a thirst for information about his or her spiritual ancestry, this book visually and vividly portrays the majestic sweep of the wonderfully rich story of the church in England. My hope is that this volume will appeal to Catholic and Protestant Christian alike and assist both communities as they celebrate their valuable contribution to the rich tradition that is English Christianity. Beyond the simple accumulation of knowledge about church history, this volume invites you to feel, see, and sample the complex tapestry of English ecclesiastical expression. Based upon more than two decades of summer pilgrimage to the United Kingdom, I leave you with a capsule history collected from my journey into England's sprawling ecclesiastical landscape.

Even though each chapter was conceived and composed as an entity capable of standing by itself, the eighteen chapters are designed as a unit. They tell the story of how a small, insignificant missionary outpost under Roman rule evolved into one of the greatest transforming forces in Western culture. For convenience and ease of comprehension, I have divided the material into three sections. Chapter one provides a chronological overview of the entire sweep of English church history. The second section pictorially focuses on the geographic centers of Christianity in England. Brief biographical sketches of significant individuals are contained in the third section. I apologize in advance for leaving your favorite figure out of this book. In tempting the reader to enjoy church history by serving up a small, seductive taste of the past, I've made no effort to please all palates by being encyclopedic in scope. Throughout the entire manuscript, photographs of the material under discussion will assist the reader in piecing together a multidimensional view of the role played by the church in English history. For would-be pilgrims and modern jet-setters, I have provided an annotated bibliography intended to direct you to some helpful travel guides and, hopefully, to that classic of English literature guaranteed to shorten a long transatlantic flight.

The time is long past when a history of the church in England could be simply a history of the glories of the saints or a sectarian trail of blood. I have endeavored, therefore, to write a popular account of English church history sensitive to the current scholarly work of intellectual historians, political historians, social historians, historians of popular movements, as well as the standard general histories of the church in England. To all of these devoted scholars, many of which are cited in the bibliography, I owe a great debt. They helped qualify my bold assertions, correct my minor inaccuracies, and question my doubtful interpretations. Nevertheless, this book makes no pretensions to rise to the level of serious historical scholarship. Therefore, my warning to professional historians: Read at your own risk!

ACKNOWLEDGMENTS

Several interested friends took the time to read all or part of the manuscript with critical eyes, adding much to its accuracy and creativity. These include two Multnomah faculty members. Professor Ron Frost pointed out several sophomoric blunders in the manuscript, and Professor Garry Friesen offered many helpful suggestions and corrections on the C. S. Lewis chapter. Kim Claassen, Amy Lineburg, and Suzanne Smith reviewed the entire manuscript and helped me with the technicalities of word processing, proofing, printing, and style. My wife Kimberly's passion for all things D. L. Sayers proved a gold mine of corrective help. Nevertheless, any errors that remain in the manuscript are mine, and I bear sole responsibility for them.

Others contributed in ways less tangible but no less important. I remember countless late-night conversations with students and alumni of the college who visited England with me. They helped give final shape and texture to this volume and I remain grateful for their enthusiastic interest in studying history by travel.

PART 1

CHRONOLOGICAL OVERVIEW

1

GENERAL HISTORY

Christianity in Roman Britain and Saxony

A first-century Roman soldier slogs his way through Northumbria on his way to the Roman garrison of Eboracum (modern day York) with his religion in his backpack. Admittedly, the rather profane image of the first arrival of Christianity in England lacks the dramatic flair of early apostolic missionary tradition. Nevertheless, this practical introduction of the faith into the cultural soil of the island dramatically transformed the course of English history for the next nineteen hundred years.

Christianity was first brought to England spontaneously by Latin-speaking invaders who served terms of service in various Roman military towns that dotted the landscape of the English countryside (fig. 1-1). Thanks to economic rough times and long unemployment lines back home in Rome, many of these career military officers were encouraged by HQ to retire and marry among the locals. As a result, an indigenous form of Christianity (Celtic), organized along monastic lines independent from the bishopric of Rome, flourished throughout England until the Saxon inva-

sions successfully forced the Celts into the historic fringes of the island (Cornwall, Wales, Scotland).

In the early years of the empire the Romans, tolerant of most religions, persecuted Christianity because of the exclusive claims it made to most people's allegiances. Several British martyrs suffered for their faith, most notably Alban, a Roman soldier put to death at Verulamium (modern day St. Albans) about A.D. 249. But the persecution ended when Constantine embraced Christianity at the opening of the fourth

Fig. 1-1. 0A part of the first-century Roman baths survive in the town center of Bath Spa in the southwest of England.

Fig. 1-2. The hauntingly beautiful landscape of Connemara, in western Ireland, witnessed the arrival of Christianity in the fourth century.

century. Free to actively engage in the broader affairs of the church, British bishops from London, York, and Lincoln attended the Council of Arles in Gaul (France) in 314. Roman Britain produced not only martyrs, but also a Christian heretic, the learned Pelagius. By teaching that man was born free of sin, possessed a free will, and had the power to choose between good and evil, Pelagius directly challenged St. Augustine's belief that man, because of his sinful nature, is completely dependent on God's grace for salvation. While the Council of Ephesus condemned Pelagius's teachings, Pelagius's ideas became popular in his native land. In order to root them out, the church in Gaul sent St. Germanus of Auxerre to Britain in 429. His mission was a success: the British Church returned to orthodoxy.

Roman political power vanished from England forever with the encroachment of Anglo-Saxon rule. Nevertheless, the recovery of Latin culture in the south came with the arrival of the missionary Augustine of Rome (no direct relation to Augustine of Hippo) by the end of the sixth century in the southeast of England (Canterbury in Kent). At that time the evangelization of the Anglo-Saxons began in earnest. Furthermore, Christianity had prospered among the Celts to the north and west. Thanks to the missionary energy of St.

Patrick during the middle fifth century, the faith spread from Northumbria to Ireland (fig. 1-2). Soon Irish indigenous Christianity was transplanted to Scotland among the Picts. In Patrick's time the island of Britain was peopled by Romanized Celts, and in its northern frontiers, by the un-Romanized Picts (Scotland). Working out of their mission station on the rocky shore of Iona, Celtic missionary scholars demonstrated a profound determination and dedication while spreading the Irish-Celtic faith to other peoples—including the ferocious Picts of Scotland. In addition, the monks of Iona sent the missionary Aidan to Lindisfarne on the North Sea near present-day Newcastle-Upon-Tyne, and Christianity was reintroduced to the northern Saxon peoples. By the seventh century, even Burgundy in southeastern France witnessed the first presence of Irish missionaries.

Fig. 1-3. A medieval illuminated manuscript from the collection at the Canterbury Heritage Museum.

12

Irish generosity extended not only to a variety of people but also to a variety of religious, intellectual, and artistic ideas. Celtic scribal art incorporated elements from ancient Coptic and pagan Greco-Roman traditions as well as from indigenous Irish-Celtic sources. Furthermore, the conventional pluriform character of Celtic Christian illuminated manuscripts set the standard for scholarship until the Carolinian Renaissance of the ninth century. So powerful was the influence of Celtic intellectual culture in Britain that even the revived Roman Catholic Christianity in Saxony (southern England) embraced the rich catholicity of Irish scholarly tradition. Accordingly, Roman Catholic Christianity, nourished by the flow of ideas from Iona's daughter monasteries such as Lindisfarne and Jarrow in Northumbria, produced beautifully illustrated Gospel manuscripts. Bede and Alcuin of York, weaned on the rich Celtic tradition, dedicated their lives to Christian scholarship (fig. 1-3). The latter was invited to Aix-la-Chapelle (Germany) by Charlemagne to establish institutions of higher learning (cathedral schools) and incorporate the study of the trivium and quadrivium (liberal arts) on the continent. As Sir Kenneth Clark, one-time curator of the British Museum, put it,

> "The civilization of antiquity . . . just squeaked through. In so far as we are heirs of Greece and Rome, we got

Fig. 1-4. The twelfth-century fortifications at Dover Castle illustrate the growing power and prestige of the Anglo-Norman monarchy under Henry II.

through by the skin of our teeth. We survived because human intelligence seems to remain fairly constant and for centuries practically all men of intellect joined the Church and some of them, like the historian, Gregory of Tours, were remarkably intelligent and unprejudiced men."[1]

Christianity and the Normans

The defeat of the Saxon King Harold at the battlefield of Hastings in 1066 opened a new chapter in English church history. William of Normandy's army, fighting under the privilege of the papal banner, not only introduced French-Norman language, law, privileges, titles, and architecture, but in addition renewed the power and prestige of the Roman Catholic Church in England. During the next three centuries, Norman influence steamrolled over the land. Norman French became the

language of the court and the educated elite while the English language was marginalized. The most lucrative clerical appointments went to men from the continent. Thanks to the establishment of "benefit of clergy" (the right of clergy to appeal litigation to ecclesiastical authority), church courts often defied the power of Royal circuit courts in criminal and

Fig. 1-5. Construction on the Cathedral at Chester began in the eleventh century.

Fig. 1-6. Windsor has grown over nine centuries into the world's largest inhabited castle.

civil matters. Nevertheless, custom dictated that the church, as a result of the beneficial services it rendered to the crown, ought to have a modicum of privileges. Even Henry II's (1154–1189) power-ful machinery of government often looked the other way when criminous clerics "got off with a slap on the wrist" thanks to lenient rulings of the ecclesiastical establishment (fig. 1-4). Henry's one attempt to bring pressure upon his "friend" Thomas Becket, the Archbishop of Canterbury, to mitigate the worst abuses of ecclesiastical jurisdiction only resulted in establishing Canterbury as the greatest pilgrimage site in all of England, thanks to the martyrdom of the archbishop. Moreover, the Norman period witnessed the production of enduring Christian scholarship. Anselm, while serving as the Bishop of Chester and the Archbishop of Canterbury, produced works of apologetic and theological substance that are still read with profit today (fig. 1-5). The martyr's blood of Becket and the logical powers of Anselm illustrate the talent and determination of the clerics that served the church in England during the Middle Ages.

Henry II's son, Richard (better known as the Lion-Hearted) served only nine months of his ten-year monarchy in England. He wasted the rest of his crown, bravely losing battle after battle to the French or the Turks on wild crusading ventures. The English nobles, desiring to be ruled by a "stay-at-home, low-tax government," directed their wrath at the next monarch, John, by forcing him to sign the Magna Carta (1215). So much for lengthy paid holidays on the continent! This conservative emphasis on preserving the rights of the church and respect for feudal (local and aristocratic) tradi-

Fig. 1-7. The magnificent walls and towers of Warwick Castle. Guys Tower, on the left, was constructed in the fourteenth century and stands 128 feet high.

tions actually helped lay the foundation for "good government" in England today.

Speaking of royals on vacation, while the extortionistic Richard II was on an Irish holiday in 1399, trying to avoid the "paparazzi," Henry Bolingbroke (Richard's uncle) rebelled and snatched the throne, ending Norman rule and placing a Lancaster in Windsor Castle (fig. 1-6). This gave Shakespeare something interesting to write about in his play on Henry V. In 1415, Henry V routed the "heavily favored" French at Angincourt (a lovely, little French country town). Unfortunately, his feeble son Henry VI blew any chances for a final English victory over the French in the Hundred Years War and was executed in the Tower of London, eventually allowing Richard III to get his grubby, murderous paws on the crown.

A fractious nobility and a weak ruler (Henry VI), along with a host of other lesser causes, plunged England headlong into civil war. Even the less-than-devout now prayed for peace and political stability. Civil war prevented the crown and aristocracy from building on a grand scale, while most of the great cathedrals and abbeys of England had been built in earlier centuries. Rather, the piety of Englishmen found expression during the fifteenth century in the building of parish churches. Responding to the increasing nationalism of the time, patrons built these churches in the uniquely English Perpendicular style, with large porches, timber roofs, richly carved choir stalls, and square towers crowned with pinnacles. The piety of the age also found expression in the endowment of chantries, a chapel in which a priest said masses for the repose of souls of the dead. Wealthy donors were normally buried in chantry tombs that rose above floor level and were surmounted by realistic effigies of the deceased. These chantry chapels reflected the many qualities of late medieval religion—its individualism, its preoccupation with death, and its reliance on the intercession of the church.

The literary production of the early fifteenth century complemented the symbolic use of pious images found in England's ecclesiastical architecture. The period witnessed the production

Fig. 1-8. The White Tower or Tower of London was constructed during the reign of William the Conqueror in the late eleventh century.

Fig. 1-9. The dissolution of monastic property, such as Bath Abbey, helped Henry VIII create a national (Anglican) church outside of Rome's control.

of two great Christian classics. As medieval mysticism lay outside the political organization of the Church, it was an area of religious life in which women could be as prolific as men. Of the great mystics of the Middle Ages, perhaps the greatest was an English woman, Julian of Norwich (c. 1342–1416). As an anchoress who lived in a cell built into the wall of a Norman period church in Norwich (St. Julian's), she wrestled with the nature of God's love, and sought to give it definition in a series of sixteen *Revelations of Divine Love. The Book of Margery Kempe,* the earliest surviving autobiographical writing in English, is the second outstanding devotional work of the period. Margery Kempe describes her struggle with mental illness, marital strife, and business failures at King's Lynn (she operated a

brewery) in unashamed detail. The book reveals the positive image of a lay Christian striving to apply theology to daily living. Today these works remain an inspiration to Christians all over the world.

During the last half of the fifteenth century, the Wars of the Roses pitted the House of Lancaster against that of York in a battle for the supremacy of the nobility. In fact, the fortunes of war fluctuated wildly when powerful nobles like Richard Neville, Earl of Warwick, helped to depose both Henry VI and Edward IV (fig. 1-7). Finally, Henry VII restored law and order, inaugurating the rule of the House of Tudor and dictating that new royal and ecclesiastical building projects would be decorated with the Tudor red-rose motif.

The last quarter of the fourteenth century witnessed a religious crisis as profound as the political crisis. The religious ideas advocated by John Wycliffe, an Oxford University scholar, were directed against traditional ideas of order, authority and lordship. His appeal to Scriptures and secular authority rather than to canon (church) law and papal authority found strong support from the anticlerical party in English politics. Secular support of Wycliffe's ideas came from John of Gaunt, the Duke of Lancaster and heir to the throne. Furthermore, anticlerical behavior (not irreligious) found expression in the poetry of Chaucer, in the Crown seizure of the wealth of the Bishop of Winchester, and

in Parliament's attempts to impose a tax on the Church. The lay followers of Wycliffe, known as Lollards, persisted as a popular force throughout the fifteenth century and, in so doing, helped prepare the way for Protestant ideas in the sixteenth century.

The Coming of the Anglican Church

Henry VIII (Tudor) was such a devout Catholic that Pope Clement VIII named him "Defender of the Faith." Nevertheless, political ambition proved thicker than church affection and soon overrode Henry VIII's religious obligations. Convinced that his loyal wife of twenty years, Catherine of Aragon, could not give birth to a son, he asked the Papal Curia to grant him a separation. When Henry's Lord High Chancellor, Sir Thomas More, refused to assist the crown in this serious matter, Henry eventually had him beheaded. When the Papacy, in turn, refused to assist Henry, he called upon Parliament to approve a divorce and formalize a separation of the Catholic Church in England from Rome. With the Parliamentary approved "English Act of Supremacy" of 1534, Henry established the Crown (himself) as head of the Church of England (Anglican) and married Anne Boleyn. Anne, like Catherine, failed to produce the much-coveted male heir, and she was sent to the tower chopping block (figs. 1-8 and 1-9). Despite four more marriages, Henry "the axe man" Tudor would never be blessed with a long-surviving male heir. Ironically, Anne Boleyn's daughter, Elizabeth I, would turn out to be one of the most powerful monarchs in English history. Elizabeth proposed a moderate, Protestant state-church based largely upon the earlier theological and liturgical reforms of her father's archbishop, Thomas Cranmer, and a declaration of faith based upon the Forty-two Articles of Edward's reign. With the help of Parliament, the queen established the "Thirty-Nine Articles of Faith" as the foundation for confessing who Anglicans worship, and the *Book of Common Prayer* as the standard form outlining how Anglicans worship. Nevertheless, the new Anglican Church proved unpopular with significant reform-minded groups within the church and Parliament. The Puritan party, for example, sought to further "purify" Anglicanism by removing from the Church of England its more "formal" and "Catholic" liturgical embellishments. Needless to say, Elizabeth rejected the reform-minded tenets proposed by Puritan leaders.

Stuart Absolutism and the Church

In 1603 the "Virgin Queen" died without an heir to the throne. Robert Cecil, the Queen's secretary, had earlier opened negotiations with the Scottish Court for the succession of James VI of Scotland. Though Elizabeth could never bring herself to name him as

Fig. 1-10. The Banqueting House near Parliament on Whitehall Road, London.

her successor, when the Queen died, Cecil successfully concluded negotiations with Scotland. The Scottish king James VI arrived in England as James I. When the Puritan party met with Elizabeth's Stuart successor James I at Hampton Court in 1604, they carried high hopes that the new monarch might be open to a further reform of the Church of England. Indeed, some foundation for change did exist. In coming to England, James I retained his title as King of Scotland with its Presbyterian state-church. Moreover, James, son of Mary Queen of Scots, schooled during his youth by Scottish Presbyterian tutors, thoroughly enjoyed advanced theological discussion. At the time, it was logical to assume that the new monarch's Presbyterian training cultivated fertile ground for his reception of Puritan theology. Nevertheless, James's enthusiastic embrace of

the episcopacy was a shock to many in England. Accordingly, the Puritans, surprised by James's icy reception of their proposals, hastily retreated from Hampton Court with only the promise of a new translation of the Bible in English (King James Version). Eventually, some of the disgruntled Puritans (particularly the Congregationalist form) found a new home for their ideas after they settled in Boston, Massachusetts.

Meanwhile, back in England, the Stuart kings (James I and Charles I) continued to irk Parliament with their Roman Catholic sympathies and usurpations of Parliament's financial prerogatives. Tensions came to a head (no pun intended) when in 1649 the monarchy was abolished and Charles I was beheaded just outside a first-floor window of the Banqueting House at Whitehall Palace (London). While awaiting his execution, Charles was able to admire the ceiling scenes of the Banqueting House, painted by Rubens, ironically depicting allegorical representations of the divine strength of the English monarch. During most of the nineteenth century the building served as a royal chapel. Today the hall witnesses no executions, just the occasional state dinner served up with elaborate security measures (fig. 1-10).

Once the monarchy was abolished, a Puritan Commonwealth led by Oliver Cromwell (one of the Puritans who hadn't left for Boston) unconvincingly

Fig. 1-11. Parliament Clock Tower (Big Ben) at Parliament in Westminster.

tians. As a result, dissenting Christians capitalized on their newfound freedom by constructing over two thousand "meeting houses" in a ten-year period.

Towards Roman Catholics there was no relaxation of restrictions. The bulk of English public opinion was zealously anti-Catholic and nonsensical stories about a "popish plot" to seize the country by violence circulated increasing local hysteria. Intolerance toward Roman Catholics continued well into the eighteenth century. According to the laws of the realm, no Roman Catholic was allowed to inherit or sell land. Apart from religious services associated with foreign embassies, Roman Catholic worship and schools remained illegal until 1791, although as the century wore on little action was taken to enforce these provisions. During the same time period, exclusion of Roman Catholic Irish from any say in the government of their own country helps account for the deep-rooted historical "troubles" in Ulster to this day.

Christianity in the Modern Period

The eighteenth century witnessed one of the greatest social changes in English history: modern mass urbanization. London's east end population swelled; massive portions of the rural populace migrated to the towns, attracted by new industrial employment. During the next century, industrializa-

guided the country. In 1685, less than two years after Cromwell's death, Charles II returned from holiday in France and restored the Crown. A relatively bloodless revolution erupted in 1688 to ward off the possibility of a Catholic dynasty led by James II. Once again the moderate Protestant reforms instituted under Queen Elizabeth were affirmed. Protestant William of Orange and his wife

Mary (James II's sister) were invited to take the crown once they had assented to the English Bill of Rights (1688). The new legislative policy quietly revolutionized the relationship between the Church of England and Parliament (fig. 1-11). Even though the Church of England's privileged position was affirmed, full freedom of worship was granted to "dissenting" Christion insidiously and irreversibly altered the texture of English society. These wretched conditions stimulated the introduction of Christian social relief programs. The late eighteenth and nineteenth century witnessed the rise of effective, evangelical social reformers inside and outside the Anglican Church. The Wesley brothers established, along with the Methodist Movement, their own ministry for the benefit of London's disadvantaged population. In John Wesley's words, "I love the poor, in many of them I find pure genuine grace, unmixed with paint, folly, and affections."[2] Following the lead of the Methodists, Christians in Parliament, such as William Wilberforce, Grenville Sharp, and Lord Shaftesbury, successfully fought for the abolition of the slave trade and the enactment of child labor reforms. The unique alliance between liberal and Christian social reformers in the early eighteenth century helped recast the country along more benevolent lines. Nevertheless, despite significant social gains for labor and the common people, urban social ills only grew in visibility. The Victorian age, emboldened with a new faith in "scientific" method, took up poverty as their next problem to solve, paving the way for a slew of government welfare programs at the turn of the century.

Roman Catholicism, since the time of the Reformation, has been made to look like a foreign or Italian intrusion into Protestant English religious life. Only in the twentieth century has Catholicism lost its exotic and dangerously sinister image. Until the Catholic emancipation in 1829—when Catholics were admitted to Parliament—Catholicism was obliged to pursue a quiet existence in country houses of the surviving Catholic gentry. Anti-Catholic demonstrations served as a recurrent feature of English life and a constant reminder of the popular distrust of Catholic religiosity. The conversions of Newman and Manning (former Anglican clerics), the sudden revival of an intellectually respectable Catholicism among writers and academics like G. K. Chesterton and J. R. R. Tolkien, has operated over the last century to restore to Catholicism a share in England's evolving religious pluralism.

The Great War caught Britain totally off guard. It scarred the British spirit by the loss of an entire generation of young men (close to a million). Hopes for a new beginning after the war were dashed as a sense of aimlessness overtook the nation's politics. The 1930s saw a depression and mass unemployment, as well as the appeasement of Hitler, led by Neville "peace in our time" Chamberlain. Nevertheless, Christianity demonstrated its continuing vitality by directly responding to the growing pessimism of the age. For example, T. S. Eliot, C. S. Lewis, Dorothy L. Sayers, and Charles Williams were Christian writers whose works of general fiction and critical apologetics gave expression to contemporary trends and values.

Notes

1. Kenneth Clark, *Civilization: A Personal View* (New York: Harper and Row, 1969), 17.
2. Quoted in Gerald R. Cragg, *The Church and the Age of Reason* (New York: Penguin Books, 1984), 147.

PART 2

IMPORTANT PLACES

2

WESTMINSTER ABBEY

Westminster Abbey deserves its claim to fame as one of England's most significant national treasures. The best view of the facade and celebrated seventeenth century towers by Sir Christopher Wren are to be found west of the abbey on Victoria Street adjacent to New Scotland Yard (fig. 2-1) and to the north across the park near the intersection of Whitehall Road. The daily operation of Westminster Abbey is a nightmare even for the most gifted of church administrators. Just imagine planning and conducting four worship services daily plus special chapels for international dignitaries, while thousands of camera-wielding boisterous tourists (3 1/2 million per year by last count) descend upon the aging abbey demanding that church officials immediately cater to their demands for souvenirs, film, refreshments, and toilets. The versatility of this structure is remarkable! Coronation hall, meeting room for House of Commons sessions, royal wedding chapel, royal and national cemetery, royal treasury, tomb of the unknown warrior, king's council, and Benedictine abbey church are just a few of the roles the ancient abbey has played during the last nine hundred years. (fig. 2-2).

Fig. 2-1. The west facade of Westminster.

For those of you who like a little gossip about the dead (mostly from tomb inscriptions and memorials), Westminster Abbey is the site for you. Best known for its royal tombs, Westminster is a great place to tread on the dead, and for a small fee they will allow you to do all the treading your little feet can handle. Furthermore, remember that the title Westminster Abbey is now a bit of a misnomer. As a result of the antipapal and neo-nationalistic policies of Henry VIII, the Benedictines were stripped of their monastic estates in the sixteenth century and as a result Westminster lost its purpose as a monastic (abbey) church. Westminster Abbey in its present incarnation was created by the eleventh-century Saxon king, Edward the Confessor. Not bad for a king who wished to be a monk. Edward established the tradition of the abbey as the burial site of English royalty. Even with the demise of Anglo-Saxon rule in England in 1066, the abbey managed to retain its role as the English hall of fame for burials and coronations. Moreover, in the late eleventh century, the new French executive officer, William of Normandy, after dispensing with "Poor Harold" at Hastings, in a final *tour de force* crowned himself king of England at the

Fig. 2-2. Ribbed vaults and Rose Window above the nave at Westminster.

high altar. The high altar, at the meeting of transepts and nave, has been the scene of most coronations and royal weddings since 1066 (fig. 2-3). Behind the High Altar, in the Chapel of St. Edward the Confessor, rests a thirteenth century Coronation Chair along with a hodgepodge of English

monarchs. A word of warning! For those hoping to catch a glimpse of the deceased Henry VIII, don't linger in the side chapels of Westminster. You may be disappointed. All Henry VIII fans should immediately head for Windsor Castle where Henry lies in state with his beloved Jane Seymour. In the far east end of the abbey stands the Chapel of Henry VII, perhaps one the best examples of late Tudor Gothic architecture (fig. 2-4). At opposite ends of the chapel lay the remains of the Protestant Elizabeth I (1558–1603) and her Catholic cousin Mary Queen of Scots. Never having had the chance to meet face to face, the monarchs, now in the eternal grip of death, have ready opportunity to discuss the merits of the act of regicide the former committed against the latter (fig. 2-5).

Fig. 2-3. The high altar at Westminster.

Fig. 2-4. The elaborate fan-vault construction of Henry VII's Chapel is one of Westminster's great treasures.

For those who have difficulty sympathizing with the acts of violence and treacheries committed by some of the more noteworthy of the dead, perhaps a stroll through the ancient cloisters will help settle the conscience (fig. 2-6). It is worth remembering that until the sixteenth century, Westminster Abbey acted as the main chapel on a large Benedictine estate that was originally located on an island in the River Thames. Thanks to both the government confiscation of monastic properties in the sixteenth century and the vast urban expansion of London in the nineteenth century, most of the original tranquility of the abbey has been lost. Nevertheless, a measure of calm may be recovered in the peaceful Cloisters. Located in the quiet East Cloister passageway, the Chapter House is one of the largest medieval chapters in England. In addition, this structure boasts one of the best preserved thirteenth-century tile floors in Europe. The Chapter served as the meeting place for the House of Commons for three centuries. To this day the government, not the abbey, administers the Chapter House.

Next door in the cloister is the Pyx Chamber. After a successful burglary in 1303, the Crown added impressive security measures, including a massive double door with six locks. Originally part of the eleventh century undercroft beneath the Monk's Dormitory, the Pyx was walled off during thirteenth century renovation to create the treasury. In addition the Office of the Exchequer, created by Henry I during the twelfth century, used the Pyx Chamber for the storing of treasury records and samples of new coinage awaiting the monthly assay (testing).

Oddly enough, Westminster maintains one of the functions for which monasteries were traditionally established. South and west of the church stands a cluster of buildings dedicated to grammar and choral education of some of England's best young male voices. As a part of their practical conservatory educa-

Fig. 2-5. Sarcophagus of Mary Stuart, Queen of Scots.

Fig. 2-6. The Cloisters of Westminster. The cloisters served a dual purpose: a covered way to the various monastic buildings and as a place for exercise. They were usually built on the warmer south side of a cathedral or abbey church.

tion, the young scholars of the abbey provide an aesthetically pleasing centerpiece for the daily sung vespers services. Founded by Queen Elizabeth I in the sixteenth century, Westminster school boasts, among its alumni, many celebrated figures in English history, such as John Locke, Ben Johnson, Sir Christopher Wren, Edward Gibbon, and A. A. Milne (fig. 2-7).

Confused or befuddled by the abbey's overlapping administrative responsibilities? You're not alone. Neither a cathedral, a parish church, nor an abbey, Westminster is a "royal peculiar" under the jurisdiction of Dean and Chapter, and subject only to the Crown. Nevertheless, Westminster is dedicated to the purpose of Christian worship and the celebration of great events in the life of the English nation.

Fig. 2-7. Southern exposure of Westminster School. Rising in the background are the south transept and the Chapter House.

3

ST. PAUL'S CATHEDRAL

G iven the tendency of a disgruntled Prince of Wales to pontificate against the ever-soaring steel and glass boxes of London's financial core, one would think that St. Paul's Cathedral was in eminent danger of being eclipsed by modern usurpers. Nevertheless, St. Paul's Cathedral remains the striking physical and spiritual symbol of London's skyline (fig. 3-1). Three churches have stood watch over this site along the north bank of the Thames River. Augustine of Canterbury established the first in A.D. 604, when he created a cathedral and diocese for central London; a crumbling Gothic structure took the second watch; the third is the classical gem we ogle today, designed by the gifted Sir Christopher Wren. Prior to the great architect's association with the cathedral, St. Paul's enjoyed a familiarity with a number of giants in English church history. For example, in the fifteenth century John Colet, the Dean of St. Paul's, recruited a young Erasmus from Holland to study under him at the cathedral school. Colet's Christian humanism profoundly shaped the course of Erasmus's academic

career. Erasmus proved the worth of Colet's instruction by serving for a time as professor

of Greek at Cambridge University. Upon his return to the continent, Erasmus continued to champion church reform along biblical and humanistic lines. The positive aspect of Erasmus's scholarship was the Greek New Testament that he published in 1516. In the preface Erasmus states,

"For I utterly dissent from those who are unwilling that

Fig. 3-1. The dome of St. Paul's looking northwest. St. Paul's is the only cathedral in England with a dome.

Fig. 3-2. The western facade illustrating its un-English style. It consists of coupled Corinthian columns topped by reliefs depicting the conversion of St. Paul.

the sacred Scriptures should be read by the unlearned translated into their vulgar tongue, as though Christ had taught such subtleties that they can scarcely be understood even by a few theologians. . . . And I wish these were translated into all languages, so that they might be read and understood, not only by Scots and Irishmen, but also by the Turks. Why do we prefer to study the wisdom of Christ in men's writings rather than in the sayings of Christ himself?"[1]

Even from across the channel, Erasmus's zeal for Greek studies set high marks for biblical scholarship, toward which some of London's native sons would

aspire. One of these was William Tyndale, whose gifts as a linguist and translator were sharpened through his academic and humanistic associations at St. Paul's, Cambridge, and Oxford. His singular skill as a translator of Scripture and his acute sense of linguistic structure served him well in preparing the most successful translation of the Bible into English prior to the coming of the 1611 King James Authorized Version. Furthermore, in the early seventeenth century London's prince of preachers, John Donne, kept the crowds at St. Paul's spellbound with his finely crafted theological discourses. Therefore, as a virtual "hall of fame" for English church history any reconstruction of St. Paul's had

to live up to the notoriety of its predecessors.

Even excepting the cathedral's notable scholars and theologians, Christopher Wren's St. Paul's differs in almost every respect from any English cathedral that preceded it—thanks to his departure from the Gothic—and is one of the largest buildings in the world. Topping out at 365 feet, the huge dome of the cathedral is second only to St. Peter's in Rome as the largest free-standing dome in Europe. Even by today's standards, the dome remains a remarkable architectural and engineering achievement.

Earning a national reputation as a talented professor of astronomy at Oxford University, Wren had already been hired by

Fig. 3-3. A view of the saucer domes above the nave floor of St. Paul's.

Fig. 3-4. The Wren at St. James is one of the fifty-one parish churches designed by Christopher Wren.

Charles II to prepare several models for the restoration of the aging Gothic cathedral. Fortunately, fate intervened. Before Wren's renovations could begin, London was scorched by a great conflagration in 1666, destroying most of the city of London. Moreover, the ancient cathedral was reduced to ashes, providing Wren with the opportunity to design a new St. Paul's from scratch. Even though the original building still had foundation segments intact, Wren blasted them in order to change even the footprints of the building. Yet controversy plagued both the design and the building of the cathedral. On the one hand, ecclesiastical authorities preferred the traditional Gothic style, while on the other, Wren drew inspiration from the more flamboyant Renaissance Italian style. Deliberations between Wren and the cathedral commissioners grew more heated. The final resolve involved compromise in a second set of plans by Wren that translated key elements of the Gothic into baroque and classical terms. The combination worked brilliantly. The shrewd architect not only received the King's warrant of approval but was allowed to make ornamental modifications as he saw fit during construction (figs. 3-2 and 3-3).

In November of 1673, work commenced on the new cathedral and continued unabated for the next forty years. Wren supervised the building, subcontracting with the finest craftsmen and visiting the site once a week. His inexhaustible

Fig. 3-5. Under the dome of St. Paul's, displaying the round Italian arches.

Fig. 3-6. St. Paul's ornately decorated ceiling and ornamental columns.

supply of energy enabled him, simultaneous with the St. Paul's project, to design fifty-one churches in the city and serve the Crown as the Surveyor-General of England (fig. 3-4). Not only did Wren live to enjoy a view of the finished cathedral from the nave, he was interred in the cathedral crypt upon his death in 1723. Only a slogan marks his humble grave: "If you seek his memorial look around you" (figs. 3-5 and 3-6).

Today, St. Paul's serves as a location for state functions. The striking beauty of the nave and choir tempted Charles and Diana to break with hundreds of years of tradition and celebrate their ill-fated nuptials in the cathedral. For a "Wren's eye view" of London, drag yourself up the 530 steps to the top of the dome. On the way up remind yourself of the less-challenging return trip. Because St. Paul's is the cathedral of the capital city, it maintains great symbolic national significance. As a working diocese, it serves as the Bishop of London's *cathedra,* or seat of authority, and acts as the ecclesiastical home of the diocese of London.

Notes

1. Erasmus in his preface to the *Greek New Testament.* English translation by Frederic Seebohm, *The Oxford Reformers: John Colet, Erasmus, and Thomas More* (London: J. M. Dent and Sons, 1867), 256.

4

HAMPTON COURT PALACE

The self-seeking Cardinal Wolsey wisely understood the strategic location that Hampton afforded on the north bank of the Thames River. As Lord High Chancellor of England, Wolsey coveted direct lines of rapid communication with the major centers of political power. His new residence met this desire, boasting direct boat service to the royal palaces at Richmond, Westminster, London, and Greenwich. Cardinal Wolsey acted as Henry VIII's chief diplomatic architect in the delicate matter of the king's divorce. The Cardinal's failure to obtain the long-desired writ of divorce from the papal curia in Rome accounts in part for his eventual disgrace and fall from power. In 1529, fifteen years after he took up residence at Hampton Court, Wolsey was forced to relinquish control of coveted palace to Henry VIII. Within a year Wolsey died. Nevertheless, the palace remained center stage during the course of the English Reformation (fig. 4-1).

Even before Wolsey's death in 1530, the king began to enlarge Hampton Court. Within six years, Henry VIII completed a great hall and rooms for his new queen Anne Boleyn ("that whore" according to Henry's faithful first wife Catherine of Aragon). Queen Anne's nuptial fortunes were directly linked to the rising fortune of English Protestantism (fig. 4-2). Rebuffed by Rome, Henry, forced to think creatively, sought the "good counsels" of Archbishop Thomas Cranmer. Cranmer's

Fig. 4-1. The brown-bricked west facade of Hampton Court. Hampton Court was extended twice, first by Henry himself and then in the 1690s by William and Mary, who used Christopher Wren as the architect.

Fig. 4-2. Anne Boleyn's Gateway is at the entrance to Clock Court.

legitimate male heir could resolve King Henry's political troubles. Henry acted quickly to depose his second wife. Realizing she could not save herself, Anne denied all charges of treason and adultery and thus preserved a chance for her daughter to one day be queen of England. According to legend, Henry VIII was chasing lobs on the tennis court at Hampton Court while the executioner lobbed off the head of Anne Boleyn. Free to marry a third time, Henry selected one of Anne's ladies-in-waiting, Jane Seymour. At last the king sired a son and the court breathed a sigh of relief.

In the Tudor apartments at Hampton Court, Queen Jane Seymour gave birth to the future King Edward VI (Edward, with the assistance of Archbishop Cranmer, introduced Protestant theological reforms to the Church of England). He was baptized three days later in the palace chapel. The Queen, robed in velvet and fur, lay on a couch receiving guests. Within another three days a severe infection in the placenta spread through her uterine wall into her bloodstream. She died within a few hours. Taken to Windsor Castle for burial, Jane's body now rests next to her husband Henry in the chapel vault. Jane's ghost traditionally haunts the palace, like that of the specter of Catherine Howard, Henry's fifth wife (executed for adultery at the Tower of London).

Although his short-lived queens have left abiding

Protestant sympathies moved him to urge a separation from Rome and the creation of an "Anglican" Church with the monarchy as titular head. The new Church severed all political ties with Rome and looked with favor upon the matter of the king's divorce (what else could it do?). King Henry's desire for a male heir was now within reach. The new royal couple, no longer limited to discreet cavorting at distant Greenwich Palace (fig. 4-3), openly flaunted their amorous adventures. Anne Boleyn's brief reign as queen (1000 days), immortalized in the design work of the inner gateway at Hampton Court, produced one of the most renowned daughters of the English crown (Elizabeth I). Unfortunately for Anne, only a memorials, it was Henry's sixth and last wife, Catherine Parr, who outlived him and enjoyed the sunniest moments at Hampton Court. Being Henry's wife must have provided an insecure existence. Keeping in mind the fate of most of her predecessors, Queen Catherine captivated her capricious husband with a natural display of wit and intelligence. Moreover, she was one of the few women of her day to publish, writing *Prayers and Meditations* in 1545. Nearly six feet tall, with auburn hair, she must have cut a striking figure at court. Less than a month after she was widowed, Catherine Parr accepted Thomas Seymour's marriage proposal and retired to Sudeley Castle in Gloucestershire (fig. 4-4). At Sudeley, Catherine continued to

play a central role in the ongoing theological and ecclesiastical reform of the country. Some of the leading clerics of the Reformation were in attendance, including Miles Coverdale, the Yorkshire biblical scholar, and the doomed Lady Jane Grey, under the direct care of Catherine herself. As a little girl, future Queen Elizabeth I found a second mother under the supervision of stepmother Catherine.

For those who are curious as to how Henry VIII acquired his amazing girth (54 inches) in the days before the invention of American fast food, the massive Tudor kitchens provide the answer. The Great Kitchen forms three connected sections with large open hearths and a serving room at either end. The serving hatches at the east end

Fig. 4-4. Sudeley Castle. Catherine Parr, Henry VIII's widow, died here in 1548.

allowed waiters access to the royal table in King Henry's Great Hall (fig. 4-5).

Throughout the history of Hampton Court as a royal

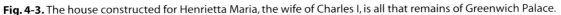

Fig. 4-3. The house constructed for Henrietta Maria, the wife of Charles I, is all that remains of Greenwich Palace.

Fig. 4-5. A view of the great kitchens at Hampton Court from the palace gardens.

residence, the palace witnessed numerous festive celebrations and conferences of state. In 1604, for example, after the accession of the House of Stuart, King James I summoned a conference here between the Puritans (reform-minded English Protestants) and the Church of England bishops. Except for a fierce outburst against Presbyterian church government (King James was an ardent Calvinist except in matters of church government), James played a neutral role. As a result of the conference's decisions, the bishops revised both the Book of Common Prayer and the Thirty-Nine Articles, and authorized a new English translation of the Bible (known today as the "Authorized King James Version"). This translation, published in 1611, proved so acceptable that it remained the pulpit and popular Bible of English-speaking Protestantism for more than three centuries. Forty-seven translators drew on the work of all of their predecessors (primarily the Tyndale, Geneva, and Bishops' Bibles) and with constant reference to the original text.

James also sought to play peacemaker with English Catholics. Earlier, when in Scotland, he had promised English Catholics greater toleration. He did not fulfill these promises due to new political circumstances. At that time, Spain deserted the Catholics of England, signing a peace treaty with England that gave no protection to English Catholics. Exceedingly frustrated by these events, a half-dozen Catholic gentlemen plotted to blow up the King and Parliament on November 5, 1605. They hired Guy Fawkes, a Catholic soldier of fortune from York, to place thirty-six barrels of gunpowder in a room beneath the House of Lords. The powder might well have gone off at the opening of Parliament had not one of the conspirators revealed the plot to the government. Some of the conspirators believed it good form to try to save their Catholic friends in the government from the violence. The conspirators, along with Fawkes, were tried and executed for treason. The Gunpowder Plot resulted in the annual celebration of Guy Fawkes Day, and promoted antipopery for a century or more. But its real significance does not end there. In fact, it symbolizes the last fling of a politically-engaged Catholicism in England. With its failure, Catholics turned away from treason and thereby made possible the existence of a respectable Catholic community in England.

Hampton Court Palace has been altered over the centuries but remains a Tudor showpiece. Furthermore, the palace serves as a visual reminder that anticlericalism lay at the center of the English Reformation. Cardinal Wolsey accumulated great powers, which he exercised in a corrupt manner certain to exacerbate the antipapalism of the English. When papal influence declined in the early sixteenth century, Henry VIII chose to ally himself with anticlerical forces in England. The wealth and pomp of the higher clergy did nothing to endear them to Englishmen. Therefore, Henry disgraced Wolsey, the cleric, and replaced him as Chancellor with a lay administration more sensitive to the rise of English nationalism.

5

CANTERBURY

The band of twenty-nine pilgrims immortalized by Geoffrey Chaucer in the *Canterbury Tales* journeyed from Tabard Inn, near Southwark Cathedral in London, to the Shrine of Thomas Becket—a journey of four days. Their ambling pace, known as the Canterbury gallop, has since passed into our vocabulary as "cantering." For 350 years, Canterbury was one of the Christian world's chief places of pilgrimage, surpassed only by Jerusalem and Rome.

The modern visitor to Canterbury can follow the path of Chaucer's pilgrims through the city, starting at the top of St. Dunstan's Street and completing the journey at the cathedral. The walk down St. Dunstan's Street to the massive Westgate towers remains little changed from the thirteenth century. Prisoners had an even better view of the imposing Westgate, completed in 1381. The sixty-foot circular towers of this town entrance enclosed the gateway and stood guard over a chamber used as a prison for condemned persons awaiting execution. Situated on the River Stour, the gateway was complete with drawbridge and portcullis. At the lower end of St. Dunstan's Street, near the towers, stand thirteen successive gabled buildings, all more than 400 years old. Readers of

Charles Dickens's novel *David Copperfield* will recognize one of these timber-framed homes as Agnes Whitfield's residence (fig. 5-1). Nearly two-thirds of Canterbury's medieval outer curtain wall survives, separating the old and new portions of the town.

Fig. 5-2. Greyfriars from the River Stour.

Past the towers and continuing to their final destination, Chaucer's pilgrims were sure to note several rickety monastic houses perched precariously along the banks of the River Stour. Franciscan friars, known as the Greyfriars, had arrived in England in 1224 from Assisi, Italy, and built England's first Franciscan friary in 1267. The Greyfriars's solitary gardens mark the site of the Franciscans' river view residence (fig. 5-2).

Canterbury Cathedral, England's most celebrated shrine, overwhelms the tiny town from all vantage points. The soaring 537-foot Gothic structure serves as home to the Archbishop of Canterbury (figs. 5-3 and 5-4). The height of the

Fig. 5-1. Westgate Towers from St. Dunstan.

Fig. 5-3. Southwest entrance of Canterbury Cathedral.

Fig. 5-5. The south transept designed in the earlier Romanesque style.

Fig. 5-4. Central tower of Canterbury Cathedral.

cathedral tower demonstrates the rising power of England's medieval archbishops. In medieval Canterbury, economic prosperity depended upon the fortunes of the Church. The cathedral and abbey, as great landowners, were a source of employment for the local labor pool. The landed properties of the Church and its wealth were the envy of royal eyes, and these desires occasionally gave rise to serious disputes between church and state.

In the twelfth century, the struggle became heated during the reign of Henry II. Henry's administrative reforms sought to limit the powerful legal jurisdiction of church courts over civil affairs. Within months after the appointment of Archbishop Thomas Becket by Henry II, a heated disagreement between the two former friends erupted over ecclesiastical legal benefits. The result of the conflict was tragic. The murder of Becket in Canterbury Cathedral is the subject of many important historical studies, but there can be no substitute for the actual words spoken by the Archbishop on that fateful day in December 1170. "I will

Fig. 5-6. Altar of Sword's Point in the north transept.

clergy's freedom from state jurisdiction and learned much in the process about the merciless power of the state. Posthumously, Becket became a martyr and a saint. Henry died a mere mortal. A portion of the cathedral that witnessed the dramatic events of the late twelfth century can still be seen in the surviving Romanesque south transept (fig. 5-5). Inside the cathedral, pass through the nave and aisles to the left where the Altar of the Sword's Point marks the site of the martyrdom (fig. 5-6).

not have the Church made a Castle," Becket announced as he ordered the monks of the cloister to open the door. Then in response to the accusations made by the four sword-wielding assassins, he said, "I'm no traitor, but a priest of God." With only one unarmed monk at his side, Becket was cut down. He had dared to clash with King Henry II over the

Unlike Chaucer's bawdy troop, modern pilgrims to Canterbury Cathedral enjoy the elaborate vaulting which fans across the ceiling of the Bell

Fig. 5-8. King's College Chapel, Cambridge.

Fig. 5-7. Fan vaulting of interior of Canterbury tower.

fully developed at Westminster Abbey and King's College, Cambridge (fig. 5-8).

Not only famous for Becket's martyrdom, Canterbury is also the mother city of the Church of England and the seat of the Archbishop. Today, more than 2 million visitors come to Canterbury each year to make contact with the unique medieval city and birthplace of Christianity in England. Today's pilgrims can still see evidence of Augustine's missionary journey to Canterbury, which brought the first seeds of Christianity to the Anglo-Saxon peoples. In A.D. 598, eight years after Augustine's arrival, the Saxon king, Ethelbert, helped him establish an abbey and cathedral church. The ruined foundations of the original structure can be seen east of the cathedral.

In the Middle Ages, the route from London to Canterbury was England's busiest road, lined with pilgrims making their way to Becket's shrine. Chaucer's explosive expose of materialism on the pilgrimage way has proved applicable to the modern tourist trade. Nevertheless, the lessons of Canterbury Cathedral and the well-preserved village in its shadow make for an awe-inspiring and endearing visit.

Harry Tower (fig. 5-7). One of the most beautiful in Europe, the ceiling of the sixteenth-century tower is a famed forerunner of the best-known vaults of John Wastell at King's College, Cambridge. Over time, Gothic architecture tended to become more elaborate. The ribs of the kitty-corner arches (vaulting) were often exaggerated beyond their function, like those in the sixteenth-century tower at Canterbury. As the Gothic style evolved, this tracery vaulting became more complex and was often creatively colored. The most overripe stage in the evolution of this style is called "flamboyant" Gothic. The English version of this style, "perpendicular Gothic," is what you see foreshadowed at Canterbury, or

6

CAMBRIDGE

Most of the affiliated colleges of Cambridge University vie for attention and distinction along a singular academic avenue that suffers from an identity crisis. Alternatively called St. John's Street, Trinity Street, King's Parade, Trumpington Street, and Trumpington Road, this thoroughfare takes its directional lead from the slowly meandering River Cam, which it borders on the river's east bank (fig. 6-1). The pastoral Cam serves as an idyllic setting to display some of the most breathtaking monuments in English educational and ecclesiastical architecture.

The modern university system located in Cambridge has its genesis in its medieval ancestor. The medieval university, like the cathedral, is one of the great architectural contributions of that age to the present. In addition, the medieval university curriculum is the forerunner of our modern liberal arts education. Medieval university studies involved seven liberal arts disciplines arranged into two subject area divisions, the Trivium (the study of the three) and the Quadrivium (the study of the four). The Trivium, the rough equivalent of the modern arts curriculum, included the disciplines of grammar, logic, and rhetoric (how to write, how to think, and how to speak). Organized under the Quadrivium, similar to our science curriculum, were astronomy, geometry, mathematics and music (how to keep time, how to construct cathedrals, how to maintain a budget, and how to speculate on the meaning of numbers). Yes, in the Middle Ages music was considered a mathematical science (anyone who has studied music theory understands this curious orientation). Having few, if any, buildings and no athletic programs, the medieval universities acted as academic guilds, which set and maintained the standards of the scholarly trades (theology, law, medicine), with the seven liberal arts serving as a foundation for all scholarly pursuits. Essentially, medieval university studies emphasized the integration of the best philosophy and science of the time (Aristotelianism) with the theology and traditions of the Christian Church. For the medieval mind, the force of argument acted to compliment and buttress the Christian faith. Anselm, an early twelfth-century Archbishop of Canterbury and philosopher of note, employed reason in the service of faith. His method has been summarized by the phrase "faith seeking understanding." So successful was this English archbishop at capturing the western imagination that he continues to be required reading at most modern liberal arts colleges. I recall that my own

Fig. 6-1. Punters on the River Cam.

Fig. 6-2. King's College Chapel from "The Backs." The Backs is the name given to the grassy strip lying between the backs of the colleges and the banks of the River Cam.

public university studies in philosophy began with reading and discussion of Anselm's Monologion (a treatise in which Anselm explores the existence of the highest necessary being deduced from the fact that beings exist). Anselm was the supreme intellectual of his age, and perhaps the finest Christian scholar since St. Augustine of Hippo.

Established in the thirteenth century by disgruntled Oxford University students and faculty, Cambridge remained a minor league institution in a minor league town until the fifteenth century when it began to enjoy royal patronage. This new source of income created several of Cambridge's most illustrious colleges. For example, the uncreatively named King's College is the proud possessor of the university's most famous chapel, a spectacular Gothic monument. Founded in 1441 by Henry VI, the college's architectural unity was disrupted by the Wars of the Roses in 1455. Deposed during the conflict, Henry's grandiose plans for the college died with him in the Tower of London. His successor, Henry VII—fresh from a victory at Bosworth over Richard III—in a fit of unbridled enthusiasm pledged himself to the completion of several pious projects begun by Henry VI, including King's College Chapel. Huge

exterior buttresses support the chapel that was constructed in three distinct stages between 1441 and 1506 (fig. 6-2). The chapel's interior consists of a single rectangular room broken only by a dark oak screen, a gift of Henry VIII. The screen bears Henry's initials and those of Anne Boleyn, his queen and second wife. One of the purest examples of early Renaissance style in England, the chapel's flamboyant Gothic beauty magnificently displays the wealth and prestige of royal patronage.

Just down the street from King's College stands the largest and wealthiest college in the University. Trinity College, established by the ever-controversial Henry VIII, is largely the architectural creation of Thomas Nevile, the Dean of Canterbury. In the late sixteenth century he demolished smaller existing buildings in order to construct the central architectural focus of the College, the Great Court

Fig. 6-3. The Great Court of Trinity College. The clock tower is on the left.

Fig. 6-4. Trinity College Library from "The Backs."

Fig. 6-5. Great St. Mary's.

(fig. 6-3). Henry's alterations involved moving the clock tower to the west end of the chapel. Fans of the film *Chariots of Fire* will be disappointed to learn that the race between Harold Abrahams and Lord Burghley, around the circumference of the great court to the cadence of the tower chimes, is fictitious. Trinity College Chapel, erected during the reigns of Mary Tudor and Elizabeth I, celebrates many of the college's prestigious alumni in its abundant monuments and statues. One of these, Sir Isaac Newton (seventeenth-century natural philosopher), was a former occupant of rooms on the first floor between the Great Gate and the chapel. According to the French philosopher Voltaire, Newton was one the greatest minds England has produced. Newton first measured the speed of sound by stomping his foot in the cloister along the north side of the court. For those more inclined toward epicurean pursuits, the college stores its well-hidden, well-stocked wine collection in cellars beneath the courtyard. Sir Christopher Wren's architectural presence haunts the courtyard at Trinity. He designed the stunning library named after him. The naturally lit Wren Library boasts the original manuscript of A. A. Milne's *Winnie-the-Pooh*. Of greater challenge to bibliophiles will be a first edition of John Milton's *Lycidas* and an eighth-century copy of the epistles of St. Paul (fig. 6-4).

Directly across the street from King's and Trinity Colleges stands the university church called Great St. Mary's. As the center of university spiritual life for six hundred years, Great St. Mary's has witnessed performances from some of Cambridge's greatest preachers. In the turbulent years of the sixteenth century Reformation, it served as a pulpit for humanistic and Protestant-minded preachers. Erasmus, Hugh Latimer, Thomas Cranmer, and Martin Bucer all propounded their "new" theological ideas at Great St. Mary's. Bucer, a native of Strasbourg and friend of John Calvin, was invited to Cambridge during the reign of Edward VI. His scholarship and moderation made him a popular Cambridge theologian. Out of admiration and respect, the University community arranged for his

Fig. 6-6. Location of academic rooms of C. S. Lewis at Magdalene.

burial in the choir of Great St. Mary's in 1551 (fig. 6-5).

North and round the corner from aristocratic Trinity lies monastic Magdalene College (pronounced MAUD-lin), established in 1524 by the Benedictines. C. S. Lewis maintained rooms here with ascetic zeal during his appointment as Professor of Medieval and Renaissance Studies in the 1950s (fig. 6-6). This phase in Lewis's academic life was also the time period when his relationship with the American writer Joy Davidman blossomed. Beyond the courtyard containing Lewis's room lies the Pepys Library. It displays the original manuscripts of prolific London diarist, Samuel Pepys (fig. 6-7). Following a distinguished political career as secretary to the admiralty and as a member of Parliament, Pepys remembered his alma mater by bequeathing his library to the college upon his death.

New England gets into the

Fig. 6-7. The Pepys Library, Magdalene College.

act at Emmanuel College (fig. 6-8). As a college closely associated with the Puritan wing of the English Reformation, Emmanuel populated the colony with some of its most gifted thinkers and rhetoricians. Well-known Americans such as John Cotton (Boston pastor and theologian), Thomas Hooker (founder of Hartford, Connecticut), and John Harvard (co-founder of Harvard University), were all alumni of the college. In his history of Emmanuel College, Frank Stubbings reports that, ". . . of the first one hundred university graduates who settled in New England, no less than one-third were Emmanuel men."[1]

Thanks to the Romans, the town of Cambridge has been around for more than two thousand years, but the university, its prize possession, got its start only 790 years ago. The rebellious Oxford professors and students who defected and established this quintessential university along the Cam gave

no thought to the charm and spectacle that have become synonymous with a Cambridge visit.

Today, Cambridge University itself exists essentially as a large bureaucracy that handles admission, the administration of degrees, real estate, and financial endowment. By contrast, it is the individual colleges within the university that are responsible for the intimate tutorials and scholarly colloquium that form the crux of a Cambridge education.

Notes

1. Frank Stubbings, *Emmanuel College: An Historical Guide* (Cambridge, England: The Master and Fellows of Emmanuel College, 1996), 9.

Fig. 6-8. Emmanuel College.

7

ELY

The plush green farmlands and dismal watery fens of East Anglia, vividly described in Dorothy L. Sayers *The Nine Tailors,* stretch toward the northeast from London, dominating the landscape of Cambridgeshire and Norfolk. Throughout the Middle Ages, Ely was an island community reached only by boat. Today, thanks to a seventeenth-century land reclamation project, the town and cathedral are a quick twenty-minute train ride from Cambridge. The landscape of the region defies logic. Surprisingly, above the low-lying fields, rivers flow between embankments engineered to catch the drain water from the swamps of the fens.

Legend has it that in the area just north of Cambridge, St. Dunstan (tenth-century Archbishop of Canterbury) saw fit to turn the local monks into eels as punishment for their lack of Christian piety—a magical transformation that earned a town nearby the name of Ely (pronounced EEL-ee). Religious propaganda aside, the fact is that St. Dunstan was a zealous monastic reformer who introduced, amid local opposition, the orderly rule of St. Benedict.

On the elevated mound at Ely, the eleventh-century Norman invaders built a magnificent cathedral from stone transported by boat across the flooded fen. The massive cathedral, nicknamed the "Ship of the Fens," dominates the skyline for miles around. Prior to the permanent stone structure, a tiny chapel served a religious community established by St. Etheldreda during the seventh century when her little

Fig. 7-1. A view of Ely Cathedral from the east illustrating the intersection of lantern tower, nave, transepts, and choir. The scaffolding visible near the central tower illustrates the ongoing program of restoration begun at Ely.

Fig. 7-2. The western facade of Ely Cathedral.

troupe sought refuge from the marauding Anglo-Saxons. According to tradition, when Etheldreda fled to the Isle of Ely in 673, she founded a double monastery for monks and nuns at the present cathedral site and was installed as the first abbess. The monastic community flourished for two hundred years until the Danes destroyed it. The Benedictines reestablished the community in 970; the new Benedictine monastic church became a cathedral in 1109.

In 1322, the original Norman tower collapsed and was replaced by the present octagonal lantern tower at the intersection of nave, transepts and choir (fig. 7-1). A view of the stately western tower reinforces the impression that this cathedral is simply a series of chapels bursting out from the masonry into rich churches of their own (fig. 7-2). Nevertheless, the real treasure at Ely is hidden inside the cathedral. The richly

Fig. 7-3. The elaborate decoration of the nave ceiling.

Fig. 7-4. The Lady Chapel.

Fig. 7-5. Buildings that form a portion of the north side of the Cathedral close.

restored nave ceiling puts to rest the stereotype of the ignorant dark ages and reminds us that medieval taste preferred brightly decorated churches

(fig. 7-3). Thanks to island isolation, Ely suffered less damage than many English monasteries during the iconoclasm of the Reformation period, preserving a piece of medieval history for today's visitor.

The Lady Chapel, built to honor the Virgin, is the largest of its kind attached to any British cathedral. Completed in 1349, the chapel originally boasted richly painted walls and the finest medieval glass. All were destroyed or damaged during the Reformation. After the Reformation, the Lady Chapel became a parish church known as Holy Trinity (fig. 7-4).

In 1986 Ely beat out Salisbury by a few months to become the first cathedral in

England to charge admission. The modest fee charged to enthusiastic tourists helps offset the cost of the ongoing need for major maintenance and repair which totals into millions of English sterling. In 1991, a comprehensive ten-year program of restoration was started at a cost of eight million pounds sterling. According to Chapter records, a guaranteed income of five hundred thousand pounds sterling must be secured each year from voluntary contributions if the future of the cathedral is to be insured. The monastic buildings surrounding the cathedral are still in use as residences, a grammar school, and shops (fig. 7-5).

To the west of the cathedral, the handsomely beamed Oliver

Fig. 7-6. Oliver Cromwell House.

Cromwell House, recently refurbished in traditional seventeenth-century style, marks Cromwell's birthplace (fig. 7-6). Cromwell rose to power during the English Civil Wars to become "Lord Protector of the Commonwealth" during the country's brief flirtation with a republic. When Charles I was beheaded on January 30, 1649, the monarchy was abolished and a republican form of government proclaimed. Theoretically, legislative power rested in the surviving members of Parliament. But in fact, the army that had defeated the royal forces controlled the government, and Oliver Cromwell controlled the army. Though called the "Protectorate," the rule of Cromwell (1653–1658) constituted a military dictatorship. Cromwell came from the country gentry, the class that dominated the House of Commons in the early seventeenth century. Cromwell rose in the Parliamentary army and achieved nationwide fame by infusing the army with his Puritan convictions and molding it into a highly effective military machine. On the issue of religion, Cromwell favored toleration, and the government gave all Christians, except Roman Catholics, the right to practice their faith. Toleration equaled state protection of the many different Protestant sects. Moreover, Cromwell advocated and obtained by act of Parliament the readmission of Jews into England. As for the Irish Catholic question, Cromwell identified it with sedition. In 1649, he crushed a rebellion in Ireland with merciless savagery, leaving a legacy of Irish hatred toward England that has not yet subsided. The state under Cromwell rigorously censored the press, forbade sports, the circus, and kept the theaters closed in England. Given the English love affair with cricket, football, Shakespeare, and the BBC, Cromwell's regime was rather short-lived. With the restoration of the monarchy came less eventful moments in Ely's municipal history. As a result, we have ample time to enjoy a relaxing afternoon in one of the towns teashops while we ponder the significant historical role played by this small town (fig. 7-7).

Fig. 7-7. An Ely tea house.

8

WINCHESTER

Sleepy little Winchester belies its former identity as the medieval Norman capital of the nation. Today, the heart of Winchester is a small, compact square bounded by the River Itchen, the cathedral precinct on the south, and a small shopping area and ruined castle to the west. Currently an overpriced center on market days, Winchester, throughout the Middle Ages, was a seat of ecclesiastical, political, and economic greatness. Here, William the Conqueror (1066–1087) established his fortified capital and William Rufus (1087–1100) consolidated Norman rule. At Winchester, Norman clerics faithfully recorded the *Domesday Book* (pronounced Doomsday), the first major census of English people and property (not a pleasant thought for the antitax crowd). In addition, Henry III (1207–1272), a native son of the city, flirted with French architecture and French women (not necessarily in that order). As a devotee of French culture, Henry III personally directed the rebuilding of Westminster Abbey in the French High Gothic style.

Conceived in twelfth-century Paris by Suger, the Abbot of St. Denis, the Gothic style reached its culmination in the French cathedrals of the thirteenth-century such as Reims, Chartres, and Notre Dame de Paris. The style was less massive than the earlier Romanesque and far more graceful. Thick walls necessary to the structural integrity of Romanesque churches were made superfluous by such Gothic innovations as the flying buttress, the pointed arch, and the ribbed vault. New churches were skeletal frameworks of stone, in which walls

Fig. 8-1. Ceiling painting in Winchester Cathedral.

served only as screens to frame huge widows of "colored" glass. The structural innovations of the Gothic style quickly spread to England where they were incorporated into the distinctive variation known as early English Gothic.

In the English style, the vaults were shorter and the interiors of the churches were often painted (fig. 8-1). The east ends of these churches (all cathedrals were built east to west, with the altar toward the east), behind the high altars, tended to be squared-off rather than rounded by apse chapels in the French manner. Generally, early English Gothic was less audacious and dramatic than the French version. It inspired the building of impressive cathedrals such as Salisbury, Wells, and Ely (fig. 8-2). Nothing quite like it exists anywhere else in Europe. The style developed through a transitional phase and marks the beginning of the three Gothic periods in English cathedral architecture (Early English, Decorated, and Perpendicular). The English cathedrals were not, as is popularly imagined, simply monuments to ecclesiastical pride. The bulk of the evidence suggests that they were products of a great common faith and of a powerful popular religious culture that embodied a singular Christian worldview. They were the highest artistic achievements of an age in which all the crafts worked toward the achievement of a shared aspiration. As Professor

Fig. 8-2. The ribbed vaulting and handsome tracery stone in the chapter at Wells Cathedral.

C. Warren Holister so eloquently writes, "The English medieval cathedrals are stone-solid evidence that romantic individualism is not the only path to artistic excellence. First and foremost the medieval architect was committed to the glorification of the Christian community above self-interest."[1] It appears from the surviving evidence that medieval cathedral builders did not believe in art for art's sake, and judging from the serenity of their monuments in stone, they were the more contented for it. As one of the few medieval stone buildings, cathedrals also served as practical structures, proving to be wise investments to the local community as multipurpose centers. In thirteenth-century

Fig. 8-3. The west facade of Winchester Cathedral with view of nave and north transept. The longest cathedral in Europe, construction began when Winchester was the capital of England. During the Middle Ages Winchester was the richest See in England.

Winchester, for example, the cathedral provided space for king's council, town hall, guild offices, classrooms, archives, choir school, market stalls, herb shop, medical research center, art museum, theater, cemetery, and tourist lodging.

Famed for its late fourteenth-century nave, the 556-foot Winchester Cathedral is the longest medieval building in Europe (fig. 8-3). The earlier Norman structure is relatively intact in the transepts and crypt, but the nave is the work of Bishop William of Wykeham (1324–1404) in the Perpendicular style (fig. 8-4). This style emphasizes vertical lines and is best illustrated by the High Altar and Great Screen located at the intersection of the choir

and transepts (fig. 8-5). In addition to some of the oldest original cathedral flooring tile, the Norman crypt contains the remains of Bishop Wykeham. He

Fig. 8-4. The nave of Winchester Cathedral.

was twice Lord High Chancellor of England and was the founder of Winchester College (1382), one of the oldest public schools for boys (fig. 8-6). Other notables found their final resting place in the tranquil confines of the cathedral. Jane Austen (1775–1817), who wrote skillfully of impoverished rural clerics, ridiculous snobs, romantic country gentlemen, and husband-hunting women, moved near to Winchester in 1809 with her family in search of proper health care for a chronic illness. Here she finalized *Pride and Prejudice, Emma,* and *Persuasion,* which first saw the light of day when published posthumously along with *Northanger Abbey* in 1818 (figs. 8-7 and 8-8).

Fig. 8-5. High Altar and Great Screen illustrating the Perpendicular design.

tenth century. The strikingly beautiful artistic illuminations (decorations) contained in the margins of the text were a project of Bishop Henry of Blois. The Bishop, in the production of the decorated Bible, spared no expense. In all, 250 calves were slaughtered to provide the vellum sheets for the text. In addition, gold was lavishly used in the marginal decorations illustrating Byzantine influence (fig. 8-9). The Winchester monastic community, endowed by the patronage of the Saxon King Alfred the Great (871–899), established a scholarly tradition that remains on display in the cathedral's ancient library. Reconstructed in 1688, the library contains 4,000 early printed books and rare manuscripts. The dignified cathedral along with its impressive ancient library holds attractions for modern pilgrim and scholar alike.

Notes

1. C. Warren Hollister, *The Making of England: 55 b.c. to 1399* (Lexington, Mass.: D. C. Heath and Co., 1971), 157.

Winchester Cathedral Library displays one of the great works of English twelfth-century art. Produced at the cathedral priory, the text of the Winchester Bible is that of St. Jerome's fourth-century translation of the Bible into Latin, commonly know as the Vulgate (the everyday Latin speech of the period). Winchester's monastics had been famed for their craftsmanship as early as the

Fig. 8-6. Winchester College students playing cricket near the ruins of the castle of the Norman bishops (Wolvesey).

Fig. 8-7. The house in Winchester where Jane Austen resided during the final months of her life.

Fig. 8-8. Burial marker of Jane Austen, Winchester Cathedral.

Fig. 8-9. The decorated initial letter "B" for *Beatus* (Blessed is the man …) from Psalm 1 in the twelfth-century Winchester Bible.

9

SALISBURY CATHEDRAL

The enduring "let's-take-our-cathedral-and-move" story celebrated in the lore surrounding Salisbury Cathedral makes for a curious footnote in English church history. Originally, the seat of the bishopric was located a mile and a half north of present day Salisbury at Old Sarum. Over the years, Old Sarum successfully functioned in turn as a pre-Christian Celtic fortification, a Roman military outpost, a Saxon stronghold, and Norman castle. The remains of the castle foundation and dry-moat may be explored to this day (fig. 9-1).

Following the consolidation of Norman rule in Wiltshire countryside, a bishopric was established at Old Sarum in 1075. A Norman basilica, begun by St. Osmund in 1092, occupied the site until friction between castle and ecclesiastical authorities over rents, judicial traditions, and precedence sent the brethren packing off to the valley below. There they established, with papal backing, a new *cathedra* at "New Sarum"(Salisbury). The ecclesiastical party had pulled out of Old Sarum "lock, stock, and barrel," literally taking the stones of the old cathedral with them to serve as building materials for the new structure (fig. 9-2).

In order to avoid a return of past conflicts, the bishop maintained dual authority as overlord of the city and the diocese. Under this arrangement the "New Sarum" quickly prospered as a mill center, receiving a royal charter in 1227. Along with the commercial prosperity of Salisbury came the addition of a spacious new cathedral structure. The nave, transepts, and cloisters of Salisbury Cathedral were constructed in the Early English Gothic style of the thirteenth century (1220–1270). The largest in England, with 190 feet of squared walkway, the cloisters were curiously never

Fig. 9-1. The ruins of the Norman fort at Old Sarum.

Fig. 9-2. The foundation of the original Norman Cathedral at Old Sarum.

On display in the Chapter today is one of the cathedral's documentary treasures—one of four surviving copies of the *Magna Carta* (1215), written in Latin on vellum (animal skin). The Chapter House, one of twelve surviving octagonal central-columned houses (along with Westminster and York Minster, functioned as the meeting place of cathedral officials (Dean, Bishop, and Wardens). While the origins of the document are well known,

used by monks (fig. 9-3). The inclusion of monastic architectural features in a secular foundation (clergy who serve the diocese) reflects the tradition in English church history of monastic orders establishing a Christian presence in the countryside. Throughout the first several hundred years of English Christianity, the regular clergy (clergy living under the binding regulations of a monastic community) dominated the ministerial labor force in England. Salisbury's episcopacy, as a late-arriving Norman metropolitan operation, deviated from this earlier Saxon rural and monastic tradition.

Other Salisbury Cathedral features are worthy of note. The impressive tower and spire (the tallest in England at 404 feet) were added in the Decorated style of the fourteenth century. The massive weight of the spire structure (6,400 tons) has required extra supports and repairs over the years. Even the services of Christopher Wren were engaged to save the old structure from collapse (fig. 9-4).

Fig. 9-3. View of the cloisters at Salisbury Cathedral.

the significance of *Magna Carta* is much disputed. It bears the seal of King John, who, suffering under the wrath of exasperated barons, affixed his seal and effectively bound himself to observe all feudal rights and privileges. Today people look back upon the decree as one of the most important documents in the history of human freedom. In the thirteenth century, this document did not introduce any new constitutional principles. It was merely an agreement between barons and the king. Admittedly, the original provisions of *Magna Carta* applied only to freemen—that is, to the clergy, the aristocracy, and town dwellers—not to the majority of the English population, who were bound to the land as serfs. The long-term significance of *Magna Carta* lies not in its original purpose but rather in its subsequent use. The later application of two potential principles in the charter, that the king is subservient to law and the king must obey the common laws of the land, played a significant role in the seventeenth-century political and religious struggle against Stuart despotism.

Fig. 9-4. West facade and tower of Salisbury Cathedral.

At Salisbury Cathedral, the curious mix of Roman Catholic and English Protestant traditions, forms, and structures reminds us that the Anglican Church was born out of the tribulations that besieged the sixteenth-century Catholic Church in England. When the English Church rejected the authority of the Pope, the church buildings and property at Salisbury, like many of the religious houses in the rest of the country, continued to be used. The Church of England, as a product of the Henrician reforms, did not reject the threefold order of church government: bishops, priests, deacons. Moreover, it continued to affirm the historic creeds and retained most of the pre-reformation liturgical structures.

Later in the sixteenth century, much of the teaching began to reflect the concerns of the Protestant reformers. As a result, the Church of England considers itself to be both catholic and reformed. Salisbury Cathedral, as a single ecclesiastical structure, reflects an image in microcosm of the larger shape of the emerging Church of England.

10

YORK CITY AND THE MINSTER

Fig. 10-2. Multangular Tower: Foundation of the wall fragment laid by the Romans in the fourth century. Later Anglo-Norman repairs and nineteenth century renovations clearly illustrated.

From the early Roman period to the present, this capital of Northumbria has played a leading role in shaping the course of Christianity in England (fig. 10-1). In A.D. 71, the Romans founded York *(Eboracum)* as a military and administrative base in Northern England. Christianity first arrived in this Yorkshire capital via Roman soldiers who brought their faith as well as their lunch with them in their backpacks. We begin our visual feast of York with a view of some the earliest ruins of this ancient capital. The ruined Abbey garden, a short distance west of York Minster, is ideal for picnics and strolls and contains a well-preserved fourth-century section of Roman wall referred to uncreatively by the locals as the *Multangular Tower* (fig. 10-2). This wall remnant not only illustrates the political importance of the region to Roman rule, but also links us to one of the most important events in the history of Christianity.

The Roman Emperor Constantine, formerly a commander of the Roman garrison at York, issued an edict of religious toleration at Milan (you know, the fashion capital of Italy) in A.D. 313. The edict not only provided Christians with freedom of worship

Fig. 10-3. Benedictine St. Mary's Abbey was built in 1089 and reconstructed in the fourteenth century. The ruins you see here date from this later period but are still more than 600 years old. In its day, St. Mary's was one of the region's wealthiest and most powerful religious foundations. As the largest wool trader in York, St Mary's exported two-thirds of all wool sent from England during the fourteenth century. By the early sixteenth century, the monasteries owned one-sixth of all English land and their annual income was four times that of the crown.

Fig. 10-1. York Minster belfry tower displays its fifteenth-century decorative paneling and elaborate pinnacles.

Fig. 10-4. The eleventh-century church, next to the gatehouse of St. Mary's Abbey, was founded by the Earl of Northumbria in memory of St. Olaf, King of Norway.

"Christian David." All that history from just a few old stones.

My favorite aspect of the garden is the ruins of the medieval Benedictine *Abbey of St. Mary's.* Formerly the major power center for monasticism in central England, York was stripped of its monastic lands during the "anti-Rome" administration of King Henry VIII. This reshaping of York's ecclesiastical landscape came about as a result of the Act of Supremacy in 1534, which separated the

throughout the empire, but also established the foundation for an enduring bond between church and state in the west. In fact, Constantine's rise to the imperial high office actually began in York, not far from this wall, when his troops proclaimed him Emperor of the Romans. Of course, it's one thing to be proclaimed emperor; it's entirely something else to actually serve in the office. The custom in those days was for Rome to fill her high office from the ranks of marauding legionary officers. So as the story goes, by the time Constantine had hacked his way to *Roma,* he had not only professed Christianity but he had also found himself knee deep in the blood of his opponents. No wonder the ancient church historian Eusebius referred to Constantine as the

Fig. 10-5. The east window (1404–1408) from the choir at York Minster has dimensions comparable to those of a volleyball court.

Fig. 10-6. The Chapter House vault at York Minster. A Chapter House is an assembly place for the governing of an ecclesiastical foundation.

cathedral in Britain, only a short walk from St. Mary's. The present structure, erected between 1220 and 1470, was preceded by the Roman fortress where Constantine the Great was hailed emperor in 306 and the Saxon church where King Edwin converted to Christianity in 627. An estimated half of all the medieval stained glass in England glitters in the walls of the cathedral. The Great East Window, constructed from 1405

Church of England (Anglican) from the Roman Catholic Church. The income from the sale of the estates was a boon to the Tudor government. As a photogenic object lesson, the broken vaults and oddly-shaped buttresses provide a stark reminder of the turbulent times of the English Reformation. While the religious economy of York was temporarily disrupted by the Tudor disillusionment, the city remained a chief export center until the eighteenth century when the city of Hull took over most of York's port functions. Nevertheless, the decline of York as an important ecclesiastical and economic center has been a blessing in disguise. Today, these strikingly beautiful medieval ruins endure as lovely abstract Gothic sculpture gardens. Furthermore, the entire ambience of old York entices modern pilgrims with its charms (figs. 10-3 and 10-4).

Everything and everyone in York eventually converges on *York Minster,* the largest Gothic

Fig. 10-7. View from the top of the central tower at York Minster.

Fig. 10-8. Flying buttresses on the south facing of York Minster. Multiple flying buttresses, one of the main characteristics of the Gothic style, are beautifully illustrated on the exterior of the nave at York Minster. These stone buttresses help shift a portion of the essential supporting weight of the cathedral away from the walls. Since the Gothic no longer relied upon the walls for the primary structural integrity, this technique allowed for much larger and lighter church structures. Medieval architects often took advantage of the Gothic flying buttress to enhance the ambience of thirteenth century cathedrals by introducing much larger windows filled with stained glass.

were not pleased. Nevertheless, the activities of the campaigning Plantagenets explain in part the friendly and not-so-friendly spirit of competition that exists between England and Scotland today. During King Edward's monarchy, Parliaments were occasionally held in the Chapter House of the cathedral. The style of the Chapter is called decorated Gothic. Octagonal in shape, it is unusual, given its size, in not having a central

to 1408, and depicting the beginning and the end of the world in over a hundred small scenes, is the largest single medieval glass window on earth (fig. 10-5).

Both Edward I (the Longshanks of *Braveheart* fame) and Edward II based their courts in York in their attempt to subdue Scotland. It goes without saying that the Scots

Fig. 10-9. View of town wall looking north toward the Minster.

column to support the massive vaulted ceiling (fig. 10-6). The Chapter House is the traditional meeting place of the Dean and Chapter, the governing body of the Minster. All canons (Chapter members) have an equal voice in decision making, the Dean being first among equals. With this in mind, each wall of the Chapter House contains six seats, making it impossible for the Dean to sit at the head of a meeting. From the twelfth century it was customary for the Dean to administer the Cathedral school and to nominate particularly gifted students to scholarships awarded by the Chapter. Thus in the office of the medieval Deanery we have the prototype of our university academic dean.

For the energetic, it's only 275 steps to the top of the central tower (figs. 10-7) of the cathedral. The Dean and Chapter of York Minster will even reward the stouthearted who brave the heights of the tower with a certificate of commemoration. Ascend to the top for a close-up view of the cathedral's stunningly beautiful flying buttresses (fig. 10-8) and the red roof tops of York city. An earlier version of this tower collapsed in 1407, so watch your step. The present tower, designed by William Colchester, is shorter than originally intended, having only its lower stage completed.

York is a fairly compact city, with most of its attractions lying within the walls or just at the edge of enemy territory. From the train station it is a

Fig. 10-10. Friendly proprietors provide a warm welcome to the Alcuin Lodge B and B in York. Many B and B's like the Alcuin are conveniently located in Bootham just a few steps outside the walls of old York.

Fig. 10-11. The Shambles, the only street in the town to be mentioned in William the Conqueror's eleventh-century Domesday Survey, takes its name from the Saxon word *Shamel*. Saxons displayed meat on benches in the *shamel*.

short walk to the town's ancient walls. The well-preserved circuit of medieval city walls (fig. 10-9) may have defended York from invaders in the past, but today the walls stand ineffectual before the multitudes of marauding hoards of tourists that descend upon York every summer. The town has retained so many of its old buildings and streets that structures dating back 600 years seem run-of-the-mill. York is justifiably a popular tourist destination, with wood-beamed medieval cottages, Victorian townhouses, and quaint bed and breakfast homes, inviting visitors to explore its ancient narrow alleyways and winding streets (figs. 10-10 and 10-11).

11

EDINBURGH

1568, Knox and his Protestant noble allies had succeeded in driving Mary out of the country. She fled to England to become Elizabeth's difficult and unwanted guest for nearly nineteen years.

A walk along Edinburgh's "Royal Mile" conveniently

A hiker's paradise, Edinburgh's historic attractions are displayed against the vivid backdrop of stark green volcanic hillsides (fig. 11-1). The city's physical geography provides a dramatic setting for the tumultuous religious struggle of the sixteenth century that shaped the destiny of Scottish history. It was within the confines of Edinburgh that the Calvinist reformer John Knox waged a verbal and ecclesiastical battle against the Catholic Mary (Stuart) Queen of Scots for the religious and political affections of Edinburgh's citizens. Knox eventually won, and Presbyterianism prospered

Fig. 11-2. The skyline of Edinburgh Castle.

amidst the narrow, winding alleys and dark huddled tenements immortalized by native son Robert Louis Stevenson in *Dr. Jekyll and Mr. Hyde*. By

displays most of the monuments linked to the course of the Scottish Reformation. At the top of a volcanic summit stands the stronghold of this Scottish capital with a magnificent view of the surrounding countryside (figs. 11-2 and 11-3). A quick look inside the castle reveals the state apartments, including the living quarters of Mary Queen of Scots and the room where she gave birth to her son James Stuart, famous for his King James version of the Bible. In abandoning her infant son by fleeing to England, Mary hoped to live to fight another day. She planned to no avail, for she never again set foot on Scottish soil. After Mary was implicated

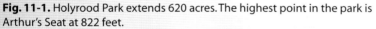

Fig. 11-1. Holyrood Park extends 620 acres. The highest point in the park is Arthur's Seat at 822 feet.

Fig. 11-3. Princes Street Gardens, located below Edinburgh Castle directly in the city center, is a lush green park where the castle's moat once intimidated marauders. Today, visitors rest on the grass and enjoy picnic lunches.

Fig. 11-4. A view of St. Giles Cathedral looking west along the Royal Mile.

in a plot to overthrow Elizabeth I, the English Queen—in true Tudor form—gave orders for the execution of her Scottish cousin. With Mary's beheading at Fotheringhay in 1587, the immediate hope of a restored Catholic monarchy in Scotland died.

Halfway down the hill from the castle resides St. Giles Cathedral, the headquarters of the Presbyterian Church of Scotland (fig. 11-4). From the pulpit of St. Giles, John Knox (1506–1572) delivered the fiery sermons that helped solidify support for the Scottish Reformation. The theological training Knox received in Geneva, Switzerland, under John Calvin prepared him well for the rigors of the clash for the control of Scotland's religious affiliations. In 1559, Knox, supported by a

group of powerful Scottish nobles, was installed as the minister of St. Giles. Even though Knox came well-fitted for the task of reformation, he was not always well-liked. Moreover, his *First Blast of the Trumpet Against the Monstrous Regiment of Women* certainly did not endear him to Queen Elizabeth's court any more than it has to modern feminists.

Fig. 11-5. The west window in St. Giles Cathedral. Stained glass was colored by the addition of metallic oxide during its burning, but usually painted afterward with delicate foliage or other detail.

Nevertheless, he played a principal role in establishing styles of worship and administration that influence the Scottish Kirk (Church of Scotland) to this day. The nearly eight hundred-year-old church of St. Giles is dimly lit by a series of spectacular stained-glass windows (fig. 11-5). The oldest parts of the present building date back to 1120.

Fig. 11-6. A view east down the Royal Mile reveals sixteenth century town homes.

Fig. 11-7. Holyroodhouse Palace. The palace remains a summer residence of the British monarchy.

stories. As a result of these practical limitations, Edinburgh boasts some of Europe's tallest sixteenth-century buildings (fig. 11-6).

The Palace of Holyroodhouse, downhill from St. Giles at the eastern end of the Royal Mile, abuts Holyrood Park (fig. 11-7). The ancient Stuart Palace dates from the sixteenth century when it served as the primary residence of Mary Queen of Scots. Many of the "soap-opera-like" events characterizing Mary Stuart's troubled regency took place within the walls of Holyroodhouse. Mary's ultimate demise had more to do with her greedy dynastic ambition than with her defiant stand against Scottish Protestantism. In an effort to solidify her Scottish inheritance and strengthen her claim to the English monarchy, Mary married her cousin, Henry Stuart, Lord Darnley. Darnley was a vicious and effeminate young man; ultimately the match resulted in a double murder and the loss of her throne. But the child of Mary

Most of structure burned down in 1385, but was quickly rebuilt. During the sixteenth century, under the leadership of John Knox, builders split the interior of St. Giles into many

Fig. 11-8. The northwest section of Holyroodhouse. One of the oldest parts of the palace, this section contains the second floor apartments used by Mary Queen of Scots. Although Holyrood Palace was restored and extended in the reign of Charles II, Queen Mary's apartments can still be seen in much of their original state, as they were at the time of the murder of Riccio.

rooms, dividing the congregation and allowing the building to be used for a wide range of purposes: school, coal store, city council chamber, police station, fire station, and a General Assembly.

A walk along the Royal Mile from St. Giles reveals some of the city's oldest structures. Because space along the Royal Mile was limited at the time, shop fronts are narrow and buildings rise to five and six

Fig. 11-9. Arthur's Seat provides the backdrop for the ruins of Holyrood Abbey.

and Lord Darnley lived to rule Scotland for thirty-six years and England for another twenty-two. A husband's jealousy ended Mary's marriage to Darnley after scarcely nineteen months. Darnley hated his wife's Italian secretary, David Riccio, and killed him in a jealous rage in the Queen's rooms at Holyroodhouse (fig. 11-8). He was "done to death" by numerous vicious dagger-wounds. Mary was six months pregnant at the time. In revenge, she connived and possibly arranged the murder of her husband on February 9, 1567. She then ran off with his murderer, James Hepburn, Earl of Bothwell. Catholics and Protestants alike were aghast at adultery and murder by a Queen, no matter how young and charming. Along the back alleys of the Royal Mile rose the cry, "Burn the whore!" In June, she was seized and forced to abdicate in favor of her fifteen-month-old son James. A year later she staged her romantic escape into England.

The ruined Holyrood Abbey, constructed during the reign of David I in 1128, stands attached to the main structure of Holyroodhouse (figs. 11-9 and 11-10). Grateful for his miraculous escape from an enraged stag while on a hunting excursion near the palace, the king determined on a philanthropic mission to endow the Augustinian Order with a home in Edinburgh. In time, the abbey came to play a prominent role in the religious life of the succession of Scottish monarchs. The abbey prospered and devoted its wealth to an ambitious architectural program during the thirteenth-century. As Edinburgh became recognized as Scotland's capital, her monarchs preferred to establish their quarters in the abbey. For example, James V, the father of Mary Stuart, like many Scottish royals before him, was crowned and buried in the abbey. His wife, Queen Mary de Guise, who reigned after his death, was also crowned in the abbey. Within its walls in 1565, Mary Stuart and Lord Darnley were married. Like other religious houses of the Roman Catholic Church, the abbey was heavily damaged during the course of the Scottish Reformation.

Today, Holyroodhouse is the queen's official home and office in her Scottish capital. She spends a week in residence there every summer, during which time she carries out a wide range of official engagements.

Fig. 11-10. The ancient nave of Holyrood Abbey is open to the sky.

PART 3

IMPORTANT PEOPLE

12

THE VENERABLE BEDE

Thanks to Bede (673–735), the English church historian, we have a fairly clear picture of the encounter of two thriving forms of Christianity in England by the beginning of the seventh century. In the writing of Bede, particularly in his *History of the English Church and People,* he describes the significant impact upon England of the competition between Roman Catholic and Celtic Christianity. According to Bede, the Celtic mission-ary Aidan founded a monastic center in Northumbria on the island of Lindisfarne just off the coast in 635, which became a focal point of Celtic Christianity and culture (fig. 12-1). In the middle decades of the seventh century, Celtic missionaries carried the Gospel south to the Anglo-Saxon kingdoms. Never-theless, it was Northumbria, above all, that witnessed the conflict and cross-fertilization of the Roman and Celtic tradi-tions. The Roman-Benedictine missionaries who had trans-planted a flourishing Roman Catholic Church to the south-east of England in Kent, coun-tered the Celtic influence radiating from Iona and Lindisfarne. Moreover, Roman Christianity, with its disciplined Episcopalian organization, elaborate bureaucracy, and ceremonial tradition, gradually advanced against the conserva-tive and loosely ordered Celtic Church.

Roman Catholic Christianity in Northumbria achieved a final victory at a synod held at Whitby in 663 in the presence of King Osway of Northumbria (figs. 12-2 and 12-3). Leading churchmen were present from all of England, representing both the Celtic and Roman Catholic observances. The particular differences between

Fig. 12-1. The coast of Northumbria near Whitby.

the churches, such as the date of Easter, clerical tonsure, and church polity, merely symbolized the more fundamental issue at stake: Would England remain in isolation from Christianity on the European continent by clinging to its Celtic customs, or would it place itself within mainstream western Christianity by accepting the traditions maintained from Rome? Even though the synodal legates concluded that the Roman way was the wave of the future, Celtic Christian culture by no means expired with the decisions of Whitby. It endured long thereafter, though little by little abandoning its separatist character.

Ironically, Anglo-Saxon ecclesiastical culture reached its zenith in Northumbria, through the scholarly center of Jarrow. Here, at the northern edge of Christendom, the stimulating encounter between Celtic and Roman-Benedictine Christianity resulted in an intellectual and cultural achievement of the

Fig. 12-3. Graveyard at Whitby Abbey.

first order. On one hand, the impressive artistic achievements of the age seem predominately Celtic in inspiration. The magnificently illuminated Lindisfarne Gospels (721) are executed in the complex geometric style typical of Celtic art. On the other hand, the great literature of the period is primarily Roman-Benedictine in inspiration. The achievements of the Northumbrian Renaissance lay in many fields: art,

architecture, poetry, paleography, and manuscript illumination (fig. 12-4). But the supreme achievement of the age was the Christian scholarship of the Venerable Bede.

Born in 672, Bede was the product of the Roman-Benedictine tradition. He spent his life under the Benedictine rule at St. Paul's in Jarrow as a

Fig. 12-4. The beginning of St. Matthew's Gospel. From the Lindisfarne Gospel in the British Museum, Cott. Nero. D. IV. f27.

Fig. 12-2. The skeletal remains of Whitby Abbey, the inspiration for Bram Stocker's *Dracula*. Dracula arrived in Whitby harbor by boat one stormy night from Transylvania.

Fig. 12-5. Durham Cathedral, reputed to be the greatest Norman Cathedral in England. It was founded by monks from Lindisfarne in 875. The current cathedral is in the Norman style and dates from the late eleventh century. Durham's thick walls, rounded arches, small windows, and solid towers evoke the feeling of strength unique in English architecture.

rare judgment. Bede was by no means a historian in the modern scientific sense and remained open to the reality of the miraculous. In so doing he anticipated the expectations of

Fig. 12-6. View of Durham Cathedral. Norman architecture, a convenient term for postconquest Romanesque (1066) in Britain, is usually considered to have run its course by the end of the twelfth century. The warlike people who gave it this familiar name were called Northmen in their day. Even though they invaded England from Normandy under their leader Duke William, they were descended from Scandinavian Vikings (Norsemen) who had settled in Northern France by A.D. 915.

superb scholar whose investigations were made possible by the fine library that had been installed at the founding of the monastery in 681. Modern scholars praise him for his *Ecclesiastical History*. Broader in scope than the title suggests, the work is the chief source of information about early Britain. Yet Bede's singular contribution to the present was in his method of historical organization—a pioneering effort. Bede possessed an acute critical sense that prompted him to use his sources with scrupulous care. He discussed the validity of his evidence, compared various sources, and exercised

Fig. 12-7. Sanctuary knocker at the north entrance to Durham Cathedral—an ornamental knocker on the door of a church which a fugitive could touch when claiming sanctuary. Sanctuary was the custom in which a medieval fugitive from justice could claim benefit and escape arrest, under ancient church law.

Benedictine). His work is an outstanding achievement, for he dealt with seven centuries of material, much of it from oral sources, and still managed to fit it together into a coherent and compelling whole. Among the remarkable sources to which Bede had access are copies of letters from the Vatican archives relating to missions among the Anglo-Saxons, as well as materials from the archive of Lindisfarne. Bede lists all the sources he used for his composition—a courtesy modern historians truly appreciate. In one of the early paragraphs in his history, Bede writes of the limits concerning his investigation:

> But in order to avoid any doubts as to the accuracy of what I have written in the minds of yourself or any who may listen to or read this history, allow me to briefly state the authorities upon whom I chiefly depend. . . . Should the reader discover any inaccuracies in what I have written, I humbly beg that he will not impute them to me, because, as the laws of history require, I have labored honestly to transmit whatever I could ascertain from common report for the instruction of posterity.[1]

Furthermore, Bede's history popularized the European practice of dating events according to the Christian era. Unlike previous ancient calendars that used the birth of cities (Roman), the reigns of

his original readers. Not wholly credulous, however, Bede submitted his work to others for editing and corrections. In addition, modern research has since confirmed the accuracy of most of his statements.

Bede's broad historical vision and his strong sense of histori-cal conscience sets his work apart from the dry hagiographic annals of traditional monastic literature of the period. His primary purpose was, in effect, to develop an historical synthesis between the multiethnic traditions in England (Celtic, Anglo-Saxon, and Latin-

Fig. 12-8. Burial place of Bede in Durham Cathedral. A sculptured quotation from one of Bede's prayers hangs on the east wall above his tomb. Designed by George Place in 1970, it says in both Latin and English:

Christ is the morning Star
Who when the night
Of this world is past
Brings to his saints
The promise of
The light of life
And opens everlasting day.

Fig. 12-9. Bede (673–735) depicted in an Elizabethan period portrait.

Notes

1. Bede, *History of the English Church and People,* trans. Leo Sherley-Price (New York: Penguin Books, 1977), 33–35.
2. R. W. Southern, *Medieval Humanism and Other Studies* (Oxford: Basil Blackwell, 1984), 3.

kings (German) or lunar cycles (Sumerian) to mark the passing of time, Bede selected Christ's birth as the great shaping and dividing event in human history. Thus the A.D. (*Anno Domini*—in the year of the Lord) system of dating was born. (The reverse dating system of B.C., "Before Christ," does not seem to have been widely used before 1700.)

Bede's legacy rests with his concept of the "English people." At a time when England was divided into many different loyalties and localities, Bede conceived of the identity of "Englishmen" and made it the central subject of his history. Buried in Jarrow at the time of his death, eventually his remains were transported a few miles south to Durham Cathedral (figs. 12-5, 12-6, and 12-7). In 1831, his bones were reinterred in the present cathedral tomb (fig. 12-8). Widely regarded as the greatest of all Anglo-Saxon scholars, Bede produced forty books on a wide variety of topics, but remains best known as a historian. Therefore it is fitting that the modern historian R. W. Southern has called him "the first scientific intellect among the Germanic peoples of Europe (fig. 12-9)."[2]

13

SIR THOMAS MORE

Sir Thomas More stands prominently as a figure symbolizing the divide in England between premodern church history and modern church history. The story of More's life and death became popular in the twentieth century through the vehicle of Robert Bolt's award-winning drama *A Man for All Seasons,* first performed in 1960. More's convictions reflected the best theology and civility of late medieval Catholicism. His vision of Christianity emphasized the continuity of tradition, the civilizing effects of humanistic learning, the support of close community, the sacramental and collective aspects of salvation, the singularity of authority, and the institutional unity of the church. Few people at that time could have predicted that, in one lifetime, the ecclesiastical world view championed by Thomas More would be reduced to a quaint and inspirational memory (fig. 13-1).

The decade of the 1530s, which witnessed England's break from Rome and the dissolution of the monastic houses, also brought about profound changes in the structure of English government. Under the leadership of Henry VIII, England became a sovereign state, owing obedience to no outside authority, with supreme power placed in the Crown and the laws of Parliament. As Professor Roberts nicely concludes, "Politically, England replaced a medieval, private, personal, privileged, and decentralized form of administration with a modern, public, national, bureaucratic, and centralized government."[1] In short, the changes in the church mirrored the revolution in English political life. During the administration of Henry VIII, the ecclesiastical power of Rome collapsed with the rise of absolute crown control over church courts, finances, lands, appointments, and benefits.

Fig. 13-1. Sir Thomas More (1478–1535), Lord High Chancellor of England.

Fig. 13-2. Plaque of St. Paul's School (east end of St. Paul's).

Unfortunately for Sir Thomas More, he was an incredibly gifted administrator born at the wrong time. His steadfast commitment to the dying old style of English Christianity not only cost him his privileged relationship with the crown, but ultimately his life. The axe fell on Sir Thomas at Tower Hill, July 6, 1535. According to popular tradition, he died "the king's good servant but God's first." While More's death failed to galvanize support for the old cause and stem the tide of civil and religious reform, history remembers him as the ultimate example of the virtuously honest government official. (On the whole, Tudor politicians were as notoriously self-serving as Presidential administrators of recent memory.)

The London-born Thomas More (1478) entered Canterbury Hall, Oxford University, and quickly became associated with the devout scholarship of the Northern Renaissance. Shortly after, he became a close friend of the great Greek scholar Desiderius Erasmus and John Colet, the distinguished Dean of St. Paul's Cathedral School (fig. 13-2). At St. Paul's in London, the three scholars actively integrated Renaissance humanism and Christian devotion. Gaining entrance to the Inns at Court, More earned distinction in the legal profession for his learning, wit, and honesty (fig. 13-3). He married the widow Alice Middleton and together they successfully raised three daughters. Unique at the time, More provided for all three girls an education in Greek, Latin, arithmetic, and music (fig. 13-4).

The popular More entered Parliament and rapidly advanced in the court of Henry VIII. Upon Cardinal Wolsey's fall from power in 1529, More was made Lord High Chancellor of England—the first time that office had been held by a layman. Henry hoped that his new, talented, and witty Chancellor might furnish assistance in the legal battle over his divorce from Catherine of Aragon. The king was wrong. When Henry seized control of the Church and divorced Catherine of Aragon, More, a loyal Catholic, resigned his office on the plea of ill health. He refused to acknowledge Henry's claim as the head of the Church in England. For this "treasonous defiance," Henry had More committed to the Tower where he remained until his execution. Eventually canonized by Pope Pius XI, 400 years after his death, Thomas More is famous not only as a virtuous statesman but even

Fig. 13-3. The Temple of the Inns at Court.

Fig. 13-5. Chelsea Old Church, rebuilt by Sir Thomas More in 1528, contains the remains of More's first wife. More intended this to be the resting place for himself and his second wife (Alice). After his execution in 1535, his head (now at Canterbury Cathedral) was fixed on London Bridge; his body was buried at St. Peter's in the Tower, but was later moved here by his daughter Margaret.

more as an author. Perhaps his best-known work, *Utopia* (1516), attacks the rich and powerful alike—whether merchant, courtier, monk, landlord, or prince. More wrote at a time when the social institutions holding medieval society together were beginning to erode. New economic undertakings were laying the foundations for modern capitalism. More realized that a way of life (Christendom) that had shaped Europe for a thousand years was passing. He wrote *Utopia* as a protest against the breakdown of the old order. At that time, thousands of people in England were being driven from their small rural claims by land enclosures to make way for corporate-style sheep raising. According to More, greed, sloth, and insatiable pride were at the root of these dislocations. To overcome the evils associated with enclosure, he proposed

abolishing private property and forming a "common" association to care for food, clothing, education, and labor. A word of caution is in order. Thomas More's reforming idealism is not closely akin to modern socialism. Rather, his utopian vision is

Fig. 13-4. The great hall of Crosby Palace, erected in central London 1466, later occupied by Sir Thomas More. In 1910 it was brought from central London (Bishopsgate) and re-erected on its present site across from Chelsea Old Church.

essentially Christian, for he locates evil in human nature, not in the socioeconomic environment. Nevertheless, like many early Christians, he did believe that pride and greed could be held in check by holding property for the common good. More's ideas were profoundly original in the sixteenth century. He maintained that materialism and private property promoted all sorts of vices and civil disorders. Since society's laws often protected these abuses, its flawed institutions were partially responsible for corruption and war. Today this view is so much taken for granted that, according to John P. McKay, "it is difficult to appreciate how radical More's approach was in the sixteenth century. . . . He towered above other figures in sixteenth-century English social and intellectual history" (fig. 13-5).[2] Yet his advocacy of social justice, judicial clemency, and Renaissance humanism notwithstanding, More was no Protestant, and because of his strong Roman Catholic beliefs he came to symbolize the last and best of the old religious order in England.

Notes

1. Clayton Roberts and David Roberts, *A History of England: Prehistory to 1714,* 3d ed. (Englewood Cliffs, N.J.: Prentice-Hall, 1991), 258.
2. John McKay, Bennett Hill, and John Buckler, *A History of Western Society,* 6th ed. (New York: Houghton-Mifflin, 1999), 437.

14

ELIZABETH I

One of England's most illustrious monarchs directly impacted the current character of Anglicanism. At the time of her coronation in 1558, Elizabeth Tudor enjoyed the youthful powers of early womanhood. From her father, Henry VIII, she inherited an athletic figure and imperious will; from her mother, Queen Anne Boleyn, a taste and aptitude for Renaissance humanism (figs. 14-1 and 14-2). At the private residence of Hatfield House some of the greatest Cambridge humanists were granted the task of educating the sharp-witted princess (figs. 14-3 and 14-4). William Grindall and Roger Ascham of St. John's College served successively as Elizabeth's tutors. By the age of ten Elizabeth was grounded in Latin and was already learning Italian and French. Her first surviving letter is one in Italian, written to Queen Catherine Parr (the one wife of six to survive Henry VIII). Under Ascham, a well-known Greek scholar, her academic talents matured. Elizabeth conversed fluently in French and Italian, readily talked in Latin, and ably composed Greek and Latin verse. Her daily studies included reading and translating the Greek New Testament, in addition to translating classical authors such as Sophocles, Demosthenes, Cicero, and Livy. Her theology was informed by reading Saint Cyprian, Saint Augustine, and the writings of the great Lutheran scholar Philip Melanchthon. According to Ascham, "Her study of true religion and learning is most eager. Her mind has no womanly weakness, her perseverance is equal to that of a man, and her memory long keeps what it quickly picks up."[1] Elizabeth was a notoriously quick and intelligent teenager.

Even as a ruling queen she did not abandon her studies. Four years into her reign, Ascham was still reading Greek and Latin to her daily and said that she read more Greek in a whole day than most clerics did Latin in a whole week. Her innate intelligence and practicality displayed itself in her choice of council members. She had the good sense to name no religious zealots to her Council. She retained eleven of the most able of Mary's advisors. Naming William Cecil as Secretary of State was particularly astute. Secular in outlook, Cecil was a moderate Protestant (he had conformed and survived as a member of Parliament under Mary Tudor), a gifted lawyer, an experienced diplomat, cautious in conduct, and in a word: prudent. Elizabeth preferred the judicious advice of eminent middle-class laymen. No step was more propitious at the opening of her reign than the wise appointment of experi-

Fig. 14-1. Greenwich Palace, birthplace of Elizabeth. The original Tudor palace on the River Thames no longer survives. Nevertheless, the Royal Naval College and the seventeenth-century Queen's House designed by Inigo Jones is open to visitors.

Fig. 14-2. Hever Castle was the childhood home of Elizabeth's mother, Anne Boleyn. King Henry VIII visited her here while staying at nearby Leeds Castle. The moat and gatehouse remain from when they were first constructed around 1270.

enced practitioners to her council (fig. 14-5).

The first significant task facing the queen was resolving the question of religion. The religious fanaticism and turmoil characteristic of the reigns of her half-siblings Edward VI and Mary Tudor had left the English nation deeply divided. Elizabeth solved the religious problem by the use of cunning compromise.

Even though Elizabeth kept her religious convictions private (something very frustrating to historians), it is plain that a desire for unity among her subjects guided her in matters of religious controversy. Her subjects' distaste for Rome eliminated the option of maintaining close associations with the Papacy. Perhaps she would have preferred Henrician Catholicism (politically separated from Rome while Catholic in theology), but that was impossible since there were not

enough Henrician bishops in Parliament to support such a scheme. Her only real alternative was to turn to Protestantism for support. Elizabeth and her Council introduced into Parliament in 1559 an Act of Supremacy and an Act of Uniformity. The first made Elizabeth the head governor of the Church of England; the

latter required every parish to use a Book of Common Prayer modeled after an earlier edition of Thomas Cranmer's Prayer Book from the reign of Edward VI. The Queen, with the assistance of the House of Commons, obtained passage of both pieces of legislation.

The Elizabethan Prayer Book of 1559, which governed the Anglican form of worship, was a compromise between the Queen's liturgical views and those of the religious reforming party in the House of Commons. As for her part, Elizabeth insisted on several amendments to the revised Prayer Book. For example, she restored the phrase "the body of our Lord Jesus Christ, which was given for thee" to the Eucharistic service, thus restoring the possible interpretation of the real presence of Christ in the sacrament. Moreover, the Queen added a rubric that required the wearing of clerical vestments. Thus, it is not overly simplistic

Fig. 14-3. Hatfield House, where Elizabeth performed her first act of state when she was crowned in 1558. The palace, partly demolished in 1607 to make way for the new house, contains mementos of her life.

to describe the church that emerged from the young Queen's revisions (Elizabeth was 26 at the time), as royalist in polity (church government), Calvinist in doctrine, and Catholic in liturgical form. Nevertheless, challenges from inside and outside the church continued to threaten the continuity of Elizabeth's religious policy for the better part of her reign.

One of Elizabeth's greatest religious challenges came from a completely unexpected source. Deposed in 1568, Mary Queen of Scots fled south to England for safety. Because Elizabeth deeply respected the idea of divine sanction associated with the regency, she expended all possible effort to achieve the return of Mary (her cousin) to Scotland as queen. Therefore, she opened diplomatic channels for the return of the exiled queen, but the Protestant Scottish protectors of Mary's infant James VI refused to accept a royal they

considered to be a murderous heretic (see the chapter on Edinburgh). Elizabeth and her Council considered it too risky to release Mary to the continent for fear that she would become the heroic figurehead of a Catholic invasion of England. Elizabeth had no choice but to retain Mary Stuart under house arrest for nineteen years. Unfortunately, the presence of Mary in England further heightened the threat of a Catholic uprising against the new Anglican Church. The northern Catholic nobles conspired with Mary to overthrow Elizabeth. These plots were quickly uncovered and amounted only to the execution of a few rebels.

The most serious Catholic threat to the Church of England and Elizabeth came not from the fumblings of the northern earls and the clumsy, careless plotting of a deposed queen, but from the powerful forces behind the Catholic Reformation (fig. 14-6). By 1580, more

Fig. 14-4. Interior of the "great hall" at Hatfield House.

than a hundred Catholic missionaries, many of them Jesuits, had arrived in England determined to return the country to the apostolic faith and the authority of Rome. Elizabeth acted decisively. In 1585, Parliament passed a bill making it treason to be a Catholic priest in England. Furthermore, the Act of Uniformity enforced regular Anglican parish attendance with oppressive fines. During Elizabeth's reign more than 250 Catholics died for their faith.

Ironically, Elizabeth's court contained crypto-Catholics and ardent Puritans. To keep them loyal she had to be above party affiliation and pursue a comprehensive religious policy. Her kingdom was Protestant, and undoubtedly, bringing disobedient Catholics into line was expedient at times. Nevertheless, she wanted no inquisitorial practices and no efforts to pry into peoples interior convic-

Fig. 14-5. Reported site at Hatfield where Elizabeth learned she was to be made "Regina" of England.

Fig. 14-6. Portrait and signature of Elizabeth.

tions. Outward conformity was enough. Under a stable and broad state-church she hoped to gradually wean her subjects away from old Roman Catholicism and new Puritan zeal.

Achieving a successful religious policy was doubly difficult because Elizabeth faced opposition from two fronts: the Puritan movement from within the Anglican Church and the Catholic threat from without. The Puritan movement originated in the 1570s among those reform-minded scholars and clerics who desired to "purify" the Anglican liturgy of its impure "Roman" practice. Puritanism cultivated the idea of a return to the pure example of early apostolic Christianity as revealed in Scripture. According to the Puritans, any practice in the Anglican Church not found in Scripture was to be rooted out.

Sixteenth-century Puritanism was no movement of religious simpletons; rather, it was an intellectually rigorous movement that attracted some of the most sophisticated scholars at Cambridge. One of these, Thomas Cartwright, a professor of divinity, adeptly criticized the English Church using the best historical and theological learning of the time. Elizabeth's administration understood that one of the real dangers of Puritanism was its close link to academic respectability. For Elizabeth, the inclination to deal harshly with Puritanism was simply a logical decision of state, quite apart from her strong, personal dislike of Puritanism (a result of her tastes, temperament and Lutheran upbringing). If she had caved in to the Puritan Party she would have ruined her policy of religious inclusion, and perhaps goaded her Catholic subjects to revolt. In appointing the anti-Puritan John Whitgift in 1583 as her archbishop, Elizabeth set her government on a course to resolutely enforce conformity to the Book of Common Prayer. The Puritans turned to Parliament for help where they garnered some support. Nevertheless, Elizabeth stood firm and defeated their efforts to establish any significant reform. By the end of Elizabeth's reign the radical Puritan separatists were few in number and the Presbyterian faction of Puritanism was in disarray. But she had not stamped out the movement completely; she had

merely covered it up. Puritanism continued to spread among learned lawyers and London merchants, remaining dormant until it rose as a powerful force during the regency of James I.

Elizabeth came to the throne when her kingdom was at war, economically depressed, and deeply divided by religion. At her death, forty-four years later, England was Protestant, the church firmly established, the Crown respected, trade expanded, and domestic peace secured. The glory of Elizabeth's reign was not that she achieved these accomplishments single-handedly, but rather that she was shrewd in the understanding of her times and wise in the stewardship of the talented officers under her command.

Notes

1. Ascham as quoted in John E. Neale, *Queen Elizabeth I* (London: J. Cape, 1959), 14.

15

JOHN WESLEY

The life story of John Wesley testifies to the concept, central to apostolic Christianity, that the true Christian life is the spiritually transformed life, not simply a comfortably religious or conformingly moral life. While John Wesley's preaching carried moral implications, it was not moralistic. Rather his teaching promoted discipline and compassion, not legalism. Essentially, his message was the radical message of the early Christians. For a proper understanding of Methodism (the evangelical movement associated with Wesley) one must remember that the eighteenth-century English revival rested upon the traditional belief of the Christian church. Wesley constantly reiterated that Methodism was no new doctrine or practice, but a revival of the old. This revival resulted from the proclamation of the gospel of grace (Christian doctrine) and was kept alive by the provision of the means of grace (Christian worship). Wesley would not depart from the Church of England. Instead Methodism created a reform movement within Anglicanism that emphasized the original tenets of Christianity. Wesley himself emphasized the historic roots of the movement in a tract written in 1786 called *Thoughts on Methodism:*

I am not afraid that people called Methodists should ever cease to exist either in Europe or America. But I am afraid, lest they should only exist as a dead sect, having the form of religion without the power. And this undoubtedly will be the case unless they hold fast both the doctrine and discipline with which they first set out.[1]

Wesley's achievements were noble and numerous. They included a fellowship at Lincoln College, Oxford University, where he taught philosophy (figs. 15-1 and 15-2), numerous theological publications, missionary service in the colony of Georgia, and ministerial ordination in the Church of England. Nevertheless, Wesley never considered these good acts as confirmation of true Christian conversion. His interaction with Moravian Christians while in Georgia led him to question his own attempts to achieve true Christian character. As a result of a futile spiritual ministry among the locals and a botched love affair with Sophia Hopkey, he returned discouraged to London. In the spring of 1738, after attending a Christian meeting in Aldersgate Street he wrote,

In the evening I went unwillingly to a Society in Aldersgate Street, where one was reading Luther's *Preface to the Epistle to the Romans.* At about a quarter before nine, while he was describing the change which God works

Fig. 15-1. Christchurch College, Oxford University where Wesley earned his B.A. degree.

Fig. 15-2. Lincoln College, Oxford University. From his rooms at Lincoln College Wesley occasionally led meetings of the "Holy Club." The club's membership was recruited from the ranks of Oxford's scholars; notable among them was George Whitefield. Lincoln College is one of the best-preserved of the medieval colleges, founded in 1427.

Fig. 15-3. John Wesley's house in City Road, London. Wesley occupied the first floor of this structure located beside the courtyard of the chapel.

Fig. 15-4. Facade of Wesley Chapel. On April 21, 1777, Wesley himself laid the foundation stone for the chapel.

in the heart through faith in Christ, I felt my heart strangely warmed. I felt I did trust in Christ, Christ alone for my salvation: and an assurance was given me that He had taken away my sins, even mine, and saved me from the law of sin and death.[2]

This turning point experience marked a new stage in Wesley's ministry that set him apart as one of England's greatest Christian leaders. Over the next fifty years he devoted each spring and summer to traveling a lengthy circuit on horseback around England (usually from London to Bath, Bristol, Chester, Newcastle,

York, Lincolnshire, and back to London) during which it has been said he preached more than 42,000 sermons, and rode more than 225,000 miles. At the end of his summer travels, he returned to his London apartment and a more sedentary ministry among the local Methodists (figs. 15-3, 15-4, and 15-5).

Fig. 15-5. John Wesley (1703–1791)

Not originally given to open-air preaching, Wesley reconsidered his methods when former Oxford classmate George Whitefield (of American Great Awakening fame and one of the most eloquent evangelists in the English Church) issued a friendly challenge. At first, Wesley disapproved of this avant-garde method of communication but once convinced it was for him, he became even more famous than Whitefield for "preaching on the highways the way of salvation."

Although John Wesley is known preeminently as an itinerant evangelist, his message was one which expressed the need for social outworkings of the gospel. In 1746, Wesley opened the first free dispensary in England for medical aid to the poor in the city of Bristol. In addition, he organized the Friends Society in 1785 to aid the urban destitute of London (fig. 15-6).

Although he earned much, Wesley never spent more than 30 pounds sterling on himself and regularly gave away more than 1,000 pounds per year (a modest fortune in that era). Moreover, Wesley loved people. He was absolutely committed to the neglected and underprivileged masses of London. Christ's foundational example of servanthood motivated Wesley's sacrificial work. The motivational foundation of Wesley's sacrificial work was Christ's example of servanthood. He regularly took time to "beg" on London's streets for unfortunate strangers and sought out wealthy members of England's aristocratic social scene, such as Selina, Countess of Huntingdon, for support of his social ministry. With the publication of his book, *Thoughts upon Slavery*, Wesley actively entered the

Fig. 15-6. Bunhill Fields burial ground in London, opposite Wesley Chapel, contains the graves of Susanna Wesley, John Bunyan, Issac Watts, Daniel Defoe, and William Blake, among other English notables.

antislavery movement, bringing the support of his Methodist followers to the side of the abolitionists. Wesley also urged the boycott of slave-grown sugar and petitioned the government for action against slavery's associated evils. Wesley's last letter, dated February 24, 1791, was addressed to William Wilberforce, a parliamentary champion of the abolitionist cause, urging him to spend his strength in "opposing that execrable villainy which is the scandal of religion, of England, and of human nature" (fig. 15-7).[3]

Notes

1. John Wesley, *Thoughts on Methodism, London, August 4, 1786,* vol. 13 of *The Works of John Wesley,* 3d ed. (Grand Rapids: Baker, 1979), 158.
2. John Wesley, *Journals Wednesday, May 24, 1738,* vol. 1 of *The Works of John Wesley,* 3d ed. (Grand Rapids: Baker, 1979), 103.
3. John Wesley, *Letters, London, February 26, 1791,* vol. 13 of *The Works of John Wesley,* 3d. ed., (Grand Rapids: Baker, 1979), 153.

Fig. 15-7. John Wesley's tomb at the rear of the chapel in City Road, London.

16

WILLIAM WILBERFORCE

The sickly little Yorkshire boy would never amount to much, or so his contemporaries imagined. The tragic, unexpected death of his father resulted in the farming-out of the young William Wilberforce to a pious Methodist aunt residing in prosperous Wimbledon, near London. Unimpressed by the evangelical influence acquired from his journey south, Wilberforce's mother returned him to Hull in Yorkshire for "safe-keeping." At that time, no one suspected that William Wilberforce would someday return to London's suburbs, not as a neglected young child, but as a Parliamentary champion of basic human rights.

Back in Yorkshire, the residue of Christian influence fading quickly, an older Wilberforce pursued a debauched life of gambling, club hopping, and social folly. In 1776, he enrolled at St. John's College, Cambridge University, more as a right of passage than for the pursuit of an academic career (fig. 16-1). In those days, attendance at Cambridge rewarded the sons of wealth with beneficial connections. After inheriting a fortune from his uncle, Wilberforce left the university for good. Nevertheless, he established significant long-term friendships while at his *alma mater*. One of these, a classmate, later distinguished himself as Prime Minister William Pitt. Moreover, one of Wilberforce's former professors at Cambridge, Isaac Milner, observed significant talent lying dormant in the gifted yet unmotivated young man. Milner invited Wilberforce to join him for holiday travels in Europe in 1784. The two killed time between the usual tourist stops by doing the unusual—reading the New Testament in the original Greek. Under the direction of Milner, William Wilberforce blossomed spiritually. Upon his return to London, Wilberforce sought out the spiritual advice of the London minister, John Newton (of "Amazing Grace" fame). Newton's combination of abolitionist reform with deep Christian commitment profoundly impacted the curious Wilberforce.

Following the example of his evangelical associates, Wilberforce, now a member of Parliament, dedicated his life to the "suppression of the slave trade and the reformation of manners in England" (fig. 16-2). The political fight was not an easy one. Opposition from conservative business interests in the House of Lords and the Commons included stall tactics designed to block antislavery legislation. Eventually Wilberforce and his political allies, including Prime Minster Pitt, gave up on the policy of securing favorable legislation by presenting evidence in Parliament of the evils of slavery. Instead, they began a

Fig. 16-1. St. John's College, Cambridge University. The second largest Cambridge college maintains a rich store of Tudor-Stuart period buildings on its campus.

Fig. 16-2. City of York. Wilberforce for many years represented York from his seat in the House of Commons.

broad-based campaign to arouse public opinion to force Parliament to act on abolition. In going public, Wilberforce drew upon the support of rational Utilitarians like Jeremy Bentham, large numbers of like-minded Anglicans, and dissenting leaders such as John Wesley of the Methodists. As mentioned previously, the last letter Wesley composed was a message to Wilberforce in 1791 urging him to not give up the political fight against the slave trade.

The support of the Christian community in the abolitionist cause was effectual and vital. In 1792, when Wilberforce called for petitions supporting his resolution in the House of Commons for the abolition of the slave trade, the Methodists alone produced more than 229,000 signatures while 21 other dissenting groups and Roman Catholic Christians produced more than 100,000 names. In 1813, for presenta-tion at the Congress of Vienna, Wilberforce and his followers gathered about 800 petitions with approximately one million signatures requesting the British government to ban the slave trade run by Europeans.

Fig. 16-3. A view of the Houses of Parliament from Westminster Bridge.

Furthermore, of the 354,000 names of dissenting Christians on petitions supporting demands for the abolition of slavery in the British Empire, 224,000 were those of Methodists. As a result of a broad coalition of support, slavery ended in colonial possessions by an act of Parliament passed just before Wilberforce's death in 1833 (fig. 16-3).

The parliamentary labor of William Wilberforce is of singular importance for the social history of England. This talented rhetorician, gifted with a beautiful voice, was a tiny, round-shouldered man with poor digestion and eyesight. After a physical and mental breakdown in 1788, he resorted to taking small doses of opium for several decades to maintain his strength and political

Fig. 16-5. The Clapham Sect held their meetings in Holy Trinity Church on Clapham Commons across the street from Wilberforce's home.

Fig. 16-6. William Wilberforce (1759–1833)

responsibilities. In spite of declining health, his gracious Christian testimony, affectionate nature, superior mental endowment, and gift of mimicry made him popular even with his political opponents. When this evangelical champion of social

Fig. 16-4. Wilberforce residence at Clapham Commons.

reform died, all of London wept.

The legacy of Wilberforce goes well beyond his political activism. Philanthropic ventures also attracted this Yorkshire M.P. (Member of Parliament). He was able to serve England in this way, through the "Clapham Sect," an association of like-minded, wealthy evangelical lay people who took residence in Clapham, a suburb of metropolitan London. He contributed large sums of his own income for various social, educational, and missionary endeavors (figs. 16-4, 16-5 and 16-6). For William Wilberforce, as with John Wesley, social service was not the end of Christianity; rather it was a product. As Professor Earle Cairns asserts,

> Wilberforce's labors on behalf of the black slaves had their origin in his experience of conversion . . . and had their motivation in the consequent love for man. . . . Black Africans were fellow creatures who should be helped rather than exploited by the white community because Christianity has equal regard for all human beings. (fig. 16-7)[1]

Fig. 16-7. Wilberforce's funerary memorial in Westminster Abbey.

Notes

1. Earle E. Cairns, *The Christian in Society: Biblical and Historical Precepts for Involvement Today* (Chicago: Moody, 1973), 124.

17

DOROTHY L. SAYERS

By giftedness and by preference, Dorothy Leigh Sayers was a scholar and expert on medieval Christianity. Her many published works give testimony to the central focus of her interests. Her translation of the *Divine Comedy* is one of the finest, with unexcelled notes illuminating the Christian meanings of the poem. *The Man Born to be King* (1941) is a series of radio plays she created on the life of Christ which displays her fine insights and her substantial abilities as a dramatist. In *The Mind of the Maker,* she is at her best as a lay apologist for essential Christian doctrine, especially the doctrine of the Trinity. A play, *The Zeal of Thy House,* composed for the Canterbury Festival in 1937, explored the sacramental nature of the creative act—that every act of creation had a triune structure which mirrored the Trinity. Her realization of the dramatic nature of Christian doctrine was to dominate her creative work for twenty years.

The outward fame and Christian notoriety achieved by Dorothy Sayers hides the difficulties faced by a lively-minded young child brought up in late Victorian England. The polite chauvinism, so characteristic of the age, limited the venues available within which talented young women could employ their abilities. Nevertheless, even with these cultural limitations, Dorothy L. Sayers's gifts blossomed early (fig. 17-1). Born the only daughter of an Oxford-educated vicar in 1893, her precociousness manifested itself in her passion for music, French literature (particularly Alexandre Dumas), and drama (her parents took her regularly to the London theater). When

Fig. 17-1. Oxford home where Sayers was born.

she was four years old, her father took charge of Bluntisham parish in the Fen district of East Anglia (the setting for her novel *Nine Tailors*). At Bluntisham, her father began teaching her Latin, which she shortly mastered. She was six at the time. A year later we hear of her reading news articles on the Boer War for unlettered adults in the parish. She demonstrated her prowess in French at the age of thirteen when she read *Les Trois Mousquetaires* in its entirety. Her abilities in French were exceptional. Being among the first group of women to receive an Oxford degree, she took advanced honors in Medieval French from Somerville College (fig. 17-2). Not content to accept employment in traditional women's professions (grammar school mistress and secretarial assistant), she sought employment in the male-dominated world of postwar London. With the return of the London expeditionary force from France in 1918, most English women were compelled to abandon their careers in favor of the returning male labor force. Not so with Sayers. Although nearly penniless (her father kept food in her cupboards by sending small sums each month) and living in a cheap London flat, she sought work in the publishing field (fig. 17-3). After months of unemployment, her fluent knowledge of French saved her when she was offered a junior administrative position at a boarding school in Normandy,

Fig. 17-2. Somerville College, Oxford University.

France. Romantic troubles ensued when she fell in love with a teacher at the facility. Her love was not returned. Longing for a stable romantic partnership, she passed through a series of unfulfilling relationships, the last resulting in an unwanted pregnancy. In order to avoid scandal to her family and damage to her father's parish ministry, Sayers kept the knowledge of her son's existence hidden by having him raised in foster care. This of course presented additional financial difficulties and forced further frugality upon her. Fortunately, the timely publication of *Whose Body?* the first in a series of financially lucrative detective novels of Lord Peter Whimsey fame, provided financial stability and support for her son, John Anthony (fig. 17-4). Partly as result of her childhood Christian training, a series of relational crises, her early financial struggles, and a deteriorating marriage (her husband suffered debilitating trauma from war wounds), Sayers returned to her Christian roots and developed her own set of religious convictions apart from the constraints and interrogations of well-meaning family members. Inspired by the refreshing portrayal of Christian thought in the works of G. K. Chesterton and Charles Williams, Ms. Sayers explored the theological beauty of Anglo-Catholicism and the rich tradition of High Anglicanism. From these sources she discovered in the Christian doctrine of the God-Man the loving stability she so longed for in human relationship. In her mid-forties now, an increasingly successful writer of detective fiction, she launched a brilliant career as a lay theologian and Christian dramatic writer (fig. 17-5).

The war years of the 1940s witnessed the height of her creative powers with the

Fig. 17-3. Sayers lived in an apartment bordering on St. George's Park, Pimlico, in her early London years.

production of her two most critically acclaimed religious works, *The Mind of the Maker* and *The Man Born to Be King*. In the former, she tried to bridge the gap between the theory of art and the theory of religion. While not primarily a theological discussion, the uniqueness of Sayers's subject matter is that it explores the possibility of a Christian doctrine of human creativity. Moreover, the work has been judged a significant contribution to academic literary criticism as it explores the relationship of the "experience" of writing a book to the writer's "completed" book. Or as Sayers suggests, "There are always simultaneously, three books: The Book as You Think It, The Book as You Write It, The Book as You and They Read It."[1] Ironically, her most controversial work centered on the story of the life of Christ. Under contract by the BBC to write a series of religious radio dramas for children, Sayers labored to produce one of our finest

examples of dramatic radio literature. Her work evolved into a highly praised and much maligned national production. The British tabloid press had a heyday with Sayers's portrayal of Christ using "U.S. slang." Numerous religious societies and churches condemned the dramatic production as "irreverent" and "blasphemous." Some ministers urged their congregations to write their M.P.'s (Members of Parliament) and even the Prime Minister in an effort to ban the plays. The negative press actually played into the hands of Sayers's production, giving it a mountain of free publicity. Sayers insisted that her presentation of Christ must be realistic and consistent with the biblical narrative. In so doing, Sayers became a pioneer figure in modern Christian drama. While Sayers was aware that her insistence on employing modern English slang in the mouths of New Testament characters offended "certain religious

Fig. 17-4. Sayers's London residence at 44 Mecklenburg Square.

persons", she insisted that "the prohibition against representing Our Lord directly on stage or in films . . . tends to produce a sense of unreality which is very damaging to the ordinary man's conception of Christianity."[2] Nevertheless, for all the great stink about the plays, the nationwide response to *The Man Born to be King* was overwhelmingly positive. Congratulations poured in from all ages and professions. When the production ended, the BBC congratulated her for providing one of the "greatest landmarks in religious broadcasting." In addition, the Archbishop of Canterbury, Dr. William Temple, proposed conferring upon her the Lambeth Degree of Doctor of Divinity for her excellent achievement in Christian evangelism. (Sayers graciously turned down the honor.)

Dorothy L. Sayers died a national figure. A lifetime of creative work proved the worthiness of such acclaim and remains as documentary testimony to her influence upon multiple fields of endeavor. Her giftedness for dramatic stage, creative fiction, crime detection, imaginative translation, biblical scholarship, and literary criticism all foreshadow developments in modern scholarship, the arts, and Christian ministry.

Fig. 17-5. The "successful" Sayers.

2. From a letter of D. L. Sayers dated February 1940, as quoted in Reynolds, *Dorothy L. Sayers,* 300.

Notes

1. From a letter of D. L. Sayers dated 4 October 1937, as quoted in Barbara Reynolds, *Dorothy L. Sayers: Her Life and Times* (New York, St. Martin's Press, 1993), 310.

18

C. S. LEWIS

Born in Belfast, Northern Ireland, this novelist, apologist, poet, and professor achieved considerable fame among an American audience for his children's stories, the beloved *Chronicles of Narnia,* and his fictional best-selling *The Screwtape Letters* (1942). The latter, purportedly written by an elderly devil, Screwtape, to edify his junior colleague in the subtle art of temptation, is the inventive and satirically humorous account of the tempter Wormwood's occupational trials and tribulations. The publication of *Screwtape* propelled C. S. Lewis into the literary world of Christian apologetics. Moreover, Lewis became well known in Britain through a series of wartime BBC radio talks. Originally published under separate cover, the radio talks were later combined into a single volume titled *Mere Christianity* (1952). These popular talks, like all of Lewis's apologetic publications, were traditionally orthodox and nondenominational in character.

Better known in academic circles for his *The Allegory of Love: A Study in Medieval Tradition* (1936), a work that traces the courtly love tradition in literature, Lewis was a fellow and tutor at Magdalen College, Oxford, from 1925 to 1954 (fig. 18-1). To this day his published critical research remains a landmark of medieval scholarship. His *Preface to Paradise Lost* (1942) was at the center of controversial debate over Milton's theological and literary interpretations. A certain dash of Platonic rationalism and philological expertise committed Lewis to exploring the intersecting relationship of image, myth, and reality. He believed that myth contained universal truth

Fig. 18-1. Magdalen College, Oxford University.

Fig. 18-2. New Buildings, Magdalen College, Oxford.

thirteenth century, and to incorporate its buildings into his new college, dedicated to St. Mary Magdalen. There, its founder established Magdalen's passion for natural philosophy and the college has maintained, for five centuries, a rigorous tradition of research in the arts. Along with C. S. Lewis, such eminent scholars as R. G. Collingwood (philosophy) and K. B. McFarlene (history) offer firm support for Magdalen's academic bragging rights.

Lewis, as a twentieth-century college don, was one of the most important teachers at Magdalen. Accordingly, he had "rooms" (living area, fireplace, furniture, sleeping and kitchen facilities) to use for conducting academic work such as reading, writing, interviewing students, and entertaining other faculty members. Lewis occupied rooms in the New Buildings (1740), overlooking Magdalen Grove Deer Park and his much-loved Addison's Walk (footpath) (figs.

and that Christianity was the archetypal myth.

For all his international notoriety, Lewis preferred the sedate parochial environs of Oxford academia. Magdalen College, where Lewis (his friends called him "Jack") was a don (tutor), has its own history, income, regulations, and

organization. Magdalen is independent and self-governing with its own set of buildings grouped around a highly manicured Victorian Gothic quadrangle. Magdalen received its foundation in 1458 by William of Waynflete, Bishop of Winchester and Lord Chancellor of England. He obtained the right to take over St. John the Baptist Hospital, which had been on the site since the

Fig. 18-3. Addison's Walk is a pathway through the college gardens named in memory of Joseph Addison, English statesmen and essayist who was a Fellow at Magdalen for fourteen years.

Fig. 18-4. Lewis's home at the Kilns, Headington Quarry, Oxford.

Fig. 18-5. The Anglican parish church in Headington where Lewis and his brother Warren attended.

18-2 and 18-3). After his conversion to Christianity in 1931, Lewis regularly attended weekday services in the College chapel. On Sundays he worshipped at his parish church, Holy Trinity, Headington Quarry, which was located in Headington Quarry close to the Kilns, his home at the time (figs. 18-4 and 18-5).

To this day, every undergraduate student at Oxford is under the direction of a don. The don lays out the course of study, advises in the selection of lectures, and holds conferences with student advisees. The academic year begins in October and is divided into three terms of eight weeks each. The autumn term is known as Michaelmas, the winter as Hilary, and the spring as Trinity. For more than 800 years, the colleges at Oxford have served as an international studies center boasting among its learned alumni the likes of John Wycliffe, Cardinal Wolsey, Sir Thomas More, Christopher Wren, John Wesley, Samuel Johnson, William Gladstone, John Henry Newman, Indira Ghandi, and Lewis Carroll. At the heart of Oxford is an intersection known as Carfax. As one travels east of Carfax one encounters High Street and in order the following colleges: All Souls, University (where Lewis studied as an undergraduate), Queens, and the handsomely towered Magdalen (fig. 18-6). Walking some distance north from Carfax, on St. Giles Street, one eventually encounters on the left the Eagle and Child Pub. C. S. Lewis, his brother Warren H. Lewis, J. R. R. Tolkien, Charles Williams, and other friends met every Tuesday, between the years 1939 and 1962, in a back room of this pub. These men, popularly known as the Inklings, met to discuss the books they

Fig. 18-6. View of High Street from the top of Carfax Tower.

Fig. 18-7. Eagle and Child Pub on St. Giles Street, Oxford, where the Inklings meetings were held.

Fig. 18-8. C. S. Lewis (1898–1963)

weekends to the Kilns in Oxford, he maintained his commitments to the Inklings (although the meeting day was changed to Monday), his relationship to his brother, and his parish church. It was during this commuting period that he eventually married Joy Davidman Gresham in 1956, an American Jewish Christian convert who had flirted with communism in the 1930s. Her tragic death due to cancer, about four years into their marriage, dramatically shaped his view on the difficulties of human suffering. Two films, both titled *Shadowlands,* have been produced on his relationship with Joy. His own trying struggle with his wife's death is published in *A Grief Observed* (1961). He served as guardian of his wife's two children until his death at the Kilns on the same day John F. Kennedy and Aldous Huxley died, November 22, 1963.

Lewis had the rare gift of translating the concepts of Christianity into the language and context of the everyday world of laymen (fig. 18-8). His characteristic warmth, reasoned wit, stunning clarity, fertile imagination, penetrating logic, and nonsectarian spirit continue to ensure him an enthusiastic readership well beyond his Church of England associations.

were writing, and, among other things, to smoke and imbibe the local brew (fig. 18-7).

After nearly thirty years of teaching at Oxford, Lewis left the university in 1955 upon the acceptance of a newly-created chair in Medieval and Renaissance English at Magdalene College, Cambridge (fig. 18-9). Lewis's commuting days began in earnest. Returning on the

Fig. 18-9. Magdalene College, Cambridge University.

APPENDIX A

HISTORY OF ENGLAND

Event	Date	English Monarch
Founding of London Christianity in England brought by Roman soldiers	60	
Death of Albans	249	
Constantine at York	300	
Romans depart England and Saxon invasions begin	410	
Patrick arrives in Ireland	432	
Augustine of Canterbury arrives in England at Kent	597	
Founding of St. Paul's in London	604	
Synod of Whitby	663	
Bede dies at Jarrow	735	
Alcuin invited to Charlemagne's court	782	
Westminster Abbey consecrated	1065	Edward the Confessor (1042–66)
Battle of Hastings	1066	Harold (1066) killed at Hastings William of Normandy (1066–87)
St. Paul's destroyed	1090	
Anselm appointed Archbishop of Canterbury	1093	William II (1087–1100)
Tower of London completed	1097	
Curia Regis and Exchequer established	1120	Henry I (1100–35)
Death of Becket	1170	Stephen (1135–54) Henry II (1154–89)
Magna Carta	1215	John (1199–1216)

Event	Date	English Monarch
Construction at Canterbury in Gothic style	1250	Henry III (1216–72)
York Minster under construction	1220–60	Edward I (1272–1307)
Old St. Paul's is completed	1280	
Parliament meets at Westminster	1338	Edward II (1307–27)
The Black Death	1348–52	Edward III (1327–77)
John Wycliffe at Oxford	1355–82	Richard II (1377–99)
Revelations of Julian of Norwich	1373	
Victory at Agincourt	1415	Henry V (1413–22)
Book of Margery Kempe	1433	Henry VI (1422–61)
Birth of William Tyndale	1494	Edward IV (1461–83) Richard III (1483–85)
Construction of Hampton Court	1500	Henry VII (1485–1509)
John Colet appointed Dean of St. Paul's	1505	
Henry VIII marries Catherine of Aragon	1508	Henry VIII (1509–47)
Fall of Thomas Wosley	1530	
Thomas Cranmer made Archbishop of Canterbury	1533	
English Act of Supremacy establishes the *Anglican* Church Dissolution of the monasteries begins	1534	
Publication of Coverdale Bible	1535	
Execution of Thomas More	1535	

Event	Date	English Monarch	Event	Date	English Monarch
Execution of Anne Boleyn	1536		Handel composed the *Messiah*	1741	George II (1727–60)
First edition of *Book of Common Prayer*	1549	Edward VI (1547–53)	John Newton's *Amazing Grace*	1779	George III (1760–1820)
Catholicism reinstated	1553	Mary I (1553–58)	William Wilberforce elected member of Parliament	1780	
Execution of Latimer and Ridley	1555		Death of John Wesley	1791	
Elizabethan Settlement	1559	Elizabeth I (1558–1603)	Catholic Emancipation	1828	George IV (1820–30)
John Knox returns to Scotland	1559		Test Acts repealed	1829	
Mary (Stuart) Queen of Scots flees to England	1568		Birth of the Oxford Movement	1833	William VI (1830–37)
Execution of Mary Queen of Scots	1587		Buckingham Palace becomes residence of sovereign	1837	Victoria (1837–1901)
Hampton Court Conference	1604	James I (1603–25)	YMCA established in London	1844	
Gunpowder Plot	1605		Charles Spurgeon converted	1850	
King James Version published	1611		William Booth establishes the Salvation Army	1878	
Pilgrims sail on Mayflower and settle in New England	1620		B. F. Westcott copublishes a more accurate scholarly Greek text	1881	
Quarrels between Charles I and Parliament	1642–46	Charles I (1625–49)	Westminster Cathedral built	1895	
Charles I executed	1649		G.K. Chesterton publishes *Orthodoxy*	1909	Edward VII (1901–10) George V (1910–36)
Richard Baxter writes *The Reformed Pastor*	1650	Birth of the Commonwealth Oliver Cromwell, Protector (1653–58)	Women win the right to vote	1918	
			The Enabling Act	1919	
The Great Fire in London St. Paul's destroyed again	1666	Charles II (1660–85)	Abortive attempt to revise the *Prayer Book*	1928	
John Milton, *Paradise Lost*	1667		D. L. Sayers publishes *The Man Born to Be King*	1941	George VI (1936–52)
St. Paul's rebuilt by Wren	1670–1723		William Temple appointed archbishop of Canterbury	1942	
John Bunyan writes *Pilgrim's Progress*	1678		Death of C. S. Lewis	1963	Elizabeth II (1953–)
English Bill of Rights	1689	James II (1685–88) deposed and exiled William and Mary (1689–1702)	Alternative Service Book accepted in the Anglican Church	1980	
			Fire at Windsor Castle	1992	
Rise of English Deism	1690s		Women are ordained into the Anglican priesthood	1993	
Isaac Watts published *Hymns and Spiritual Songs*	1707	Anne (1702–14)			
Jonathan Swift, *Gulliver's Travel's*	1726	George I (1714–27)			

APPENDIX B

VISITING ENGLISH ECCLESIASTICAL SITES

The major historical sites featured in the chapters of this book are easily covered in a two-week visit to the U.K. provided you have a rail pass and are without children. Traveling with children? Parents remain sane by cutting the itinerary in half allowing for a less aggressive pace. Flying from the west coast of the United States? Remember to allow three days just for air travel. London is on Greenwich Mean Time (GTM). Which means you arrive in London the day after your flight departs from Portland, Oregon.

For those on limited schedules here are my suggestions for one and two-day London stays. One day visit: St. Paul's Cathedral and Westminster Abbey. Enjoy evensong at Westminster. Both churches are must items for serious ecclesiastical history buffs. Two day visit: Same as above for day one. On the second day add a day trip from London to either Canterbury Cathedral (90 minutes by train) or Hampton Court (30 minutes by train).

Favorite Ecclesiastical Sites in Britain

Consider organizing your two- or three-week trip with a visit to these memorable church history sites.

- *Cathedrals*: Canterbury, Durham, St. Paul's, Wells, Yorkminster
- *Ruined Abbeys*: Rievaulx, Fountains (Both in Yorkshire)
- *Holy Islands*: Iona (Inner Hebrides), Lindesfarne (near Newcastle)
- *Chapels*: King's College Chapel (Cambridge), St. George's Chapel (Windsor), Chapel of St. John (Tower of London), Wesley Chapel (London)
- *Royal Peculiar*: Westminster Abbey
- *Parish Churches*: St. Stephen Walbrook (London), The Wren at St. James (London), Holy Trinity Headington Quarry (Oxford) Bath Abbey (Bath)

Famous London "Resting Places"

Anne Boleyn
Chapel of St. Peter (Tower)

John Bunyan
Bunhill Fields on City Rd.

Charles I
St. George's Chapel (Windsor)

Geoffrey Chaucer
Westminster Abbey

Anne of Cleves
Westminster Abbey

Daniel Defoe
Bunhill Fields on City Rd.

John Donne
St. Paul's Cathedral
Elizabeth I

Westminster Abbey

John Foxe
St. Giles Cripplegate

Henry VIII
St. George's Chapel (Windsor)

Catherine Howard
Chapel of St. Peter (Tower)

John Milton
St. Giles Cripplegate

Sir Thomas More
Cheyne Walk, Old Church (Chelsea)

Lord Nelson
St. Paul's Cathedral

Samuel Pepys
St. Olave's in Hart St.

Mary Stuart (Queen of Scots)
Westminster Abbey

Isaac Watts
Bunhill Fields on City Rd.

William Wilberforce
Westminster Abbey

Susannah Wesley
Bunhill Fields on City Rd.

John Wesley
Wesley Chapel on City Rd.

Etiquette

American tourists still have a reputation for rudeness by British standards and should avoid glaring mistakes like bringing food into a church, snapping pictures during services, and insisting on ice water in a restaurant. Be as polite as possible when asking for something. During conversation refer to people as British, as opposed to English, Scottish or Welsh. Remember not everyone living in England is English.

Photography

Interior flash photography is prohibited at all cathedrals in the country. Most cathedral governing boards require that you make written arrangements for non-flash interior photography. This usually consists of a small fee and application for permit. Consult local cathedral officials for arrangements.

Buy a supply of film before you leave: it's more expensive in the U.K. Pack an extra battery for your built in light meter. Unless you're shooting with 1000 ASA or more, airport security ex-rays will not harm your pictures. After two-dozen trips to Europe and thousands of slides, I have never experienced over-development of film due to airport security.

Credit Cards and ATMs

Credit cards are widely accepted throughout Britain. Automated Teller Machines (ATMs), known as "holes-in-the-wall" because of the ease with which they can be ripped out of a wall, are rapidly multiplying in Britain. Your home bank will convert your withdrawal into your home currency at a "fair" rate. A PIN (personal identification number) is essential for ATM use. I have used ATMs throughout Britain with no problems. They operate just like the U.S. ATMs. The British pound sterling is divided into 100 pence (100p.).

Observe, however, that the 1 pound note has been replaced with a heavy gold coin. A "quid" is 1 pound. *Exchange: US$ = 0.67 British pounds, 1 pound = US $1.60. *rates change daily.

Climate

When choosing clothing, remember that London, while usually wet, stays fairly mild, with an average summer temperature in the mid-60's to low-70's. May and June are the sunniest months, July and August the warmest (78 being a "real scorcher"). Throughout the year, you should expect unstable weather patterns; a bright and cloudless morning sky often precedes intermittent afternoon showers. Northern England will be 2 to 5 degrees cooler with greater chance of rain. Winters are cool and damp.

Packing

Don't indulge. Pack light. Leave the wedding photographs, the CD collection, and the three piece suit where they belong—at home. The more ground you're planning to cover abroad, the lighter you ought to travel. You will quickly find that the convenience of having less to carry far outweighs the inconvenience of a small wardrobe. You simply won't need as much clothing as you think. Organize your travel wardrobe around a single color that allows you to mix, match, and layer clothes. Use laundries to renew your wardrobe. Consider loose-fitting clothes that do not wrinkle.

Safety and Security

London is a tourist-friendly city, much safer than our major U.S. cities of equal size.

Safety tips: (1)Don't leave your packages unattended on the underground, buses, or trains. Packages will be taken, either by thieves or the police, who are paranoid—and rightly so—about IRA bombs. The greatest danger in your trip lies not in explosions but in inconvenience caused by security alerts. (2)A lesser-known but very real source of danger to foreign pedestrians in London is crossing the street. Despite the prominent "look right" signs, at least one American dies every year after looking the wrong way before stepping into the road.

Speaking British (Briefly!)

biscuit	if sweet, a cookie; if not, a cracker
cheers	thank you, good-bye
chips	french fries
concession	discount on admission
crisps	potato chips
ensuite	with bath
fag	cigarette
fortnight	two weeks
hire	rental
lift	elevator
loo	rest room
lorry	truck
mind	watch (as in watch your step)
private school	public school
queue	a line
way out	exit
W.C.	rest room

BIBLIOGRAPHY

What to Read in Your Local Library

Backhouse, Janet. *The Lindisfarne Gospels.* San Francisco: Chronicle Books, 1993. This book describes how the manuscript was made, placing it in the context of Christian Northumbria.

Barlow, Frank. *Thomas Becket.* Berkeley: University of California, 1986. This work masterfully recounts the life of this contentious figure, using scholarly detail to de-romanticize the twelfth-century church.

Bebbington, David. *Evangelicalism in Modern Britain: A History from the 1730s to the 1980s.* Grand Rapids: Baker, 1992. This book carefully surveys how the evangelical movement has been molded by its English environment.

Bede. *A History of the English Church and People.* New York: Penguin, 1956. This is a work of art and a fundamental source for the history of Anglo-Saxon England.

Bettey, J. H. *Church and Community: The Parish Church in English Life.* New York: Barnes and Noble, 1979. It explores eighteenth-century religiosity on the local level.

Brown, Peter, ed. *The Book of Kells.* New York: Thames and Hudson, 1980. The book supplies forty-eight detailed pages in color from the manuscript in Trinity College, Dublin.

Cahill, Thomas. *How the Irish Saved Civilization: The Untold Story of Ireland's Heroic Role from the Fall of Rome to the Rise of Medieval Europe.* New York: Doubleday, 1995. This work serves up a delightful and illuminating look into the treasury of Celtic culture.

Cairns, E. E. *Christianity Through the Centuries.* Grand Rapids: Zondervan, 1996. A broad synthesis of church history with specialized chapters on England by a veteran scholar.

Collinson, P. *The Religion of Protestants: The Church in English Society, 1559–1625.* Oxford: Clarendon Press, 1982. It portrays a church in which there was room for Puritans until Archbishop Laud appeared on the scene.

Cragg, G. R. *The Church in the Age of Reason, 1648–1789.* New York: Penguin, 1960. This book shatters the supposition that early modern English Christianity was moribund and anti-intellectual.

Dickens, A. G. *The English Reformation.* New York: Schoken Books, 1964. The fundamental starting point for English Reformation studies.

Edwards, David L. *A Concise History of English Christianity: From Roman Times to the Present Day.* London: HarperCollins, 1998. It documents the profound influence of Christianity upon the social, cultural, and political development of England.

Fraser, Antonia. *Mary Queen of Scots.* London: Weidenfeld and Nicholson, 1969. The book compassionately illuminates one of the most fascinating figures in European history.

——— . *The Six Wives of Henry VIII.* London: Weidenfeld and Nicholson, 1992. A detailed coverage of the marital trials of Henry VIII.

Haskins, Charles H. *The Rise of the Universities.* New York: Great Seal Books, 1957. A witty series of lectures on the origin and nature of the earliest universities.

Hill, Christopher. *God's Englishman: Oliver Cromwell and the English Revolution.* London: Weidenfeld and Nicholson, 1970. This book provides us with a sympathetic and informative guide to Cromwell.

Hollister, Charles W. *The Making of England, 55 b.c.–1399.* Lexington, Massachusetts: D. C. Heath, 1966. This work surveys the history of England up to the fourteenth century with plenty of space devoted to the church.

Howarth, David. *1066: The Year of Conquest.* New York: Penguin, 1981. A lively and cleverly written account of the Norman invasion of England from Norman, Scandinavian, and Anglo-Saxon perspectives.

Ives, Eric W. *Anne Boleyn.* New York: Blackwell, 1986. It splendidly portrays Anne as sophisticated, outspoken, and a friend of humanists.

Knowles, David. *Bare Ruined Choirs: The Dissolution of the English Monasteries.* New York: Cambridge University Press, 1976. This title brilliantly illustrates the dissolution of the English monasteries.

——— . *The Monastic Order in England.* Cambridge: Cambridge University Press, 1963. This work skillfully traces the evolution of early medieval English monasticism.

Macaulay, David. *Cathedral: The Story of Its Construction.* Boston: Houghton Mifflin, 1973. An exploration of the engineering problems involved in cathedral buildings and places the subject within its social context.

MacCulloch, Diarmaid. *Thomas Cranmer.* New Haven: Yale University Press, 1996. A definitive biography of the most controversial bigwig in the history of the English Church.

Marius, Richard. *Thomas More: A Biography.* New York: Knopf, 1984. This title explores the fascinating character and career of this English Christian humanist.

Mattingly, Garrett. *The Armada.* Boston: Houghton Mifflin, 1959. Tells the exciting tale of the English defeat of the Spanish naval invasion.

Mayr-Harting, Henry. *The Coming of Christianity to Anglo-Saxon England.* Third edition. University Park: Pennsylvania State University, 1991. Elegantly treats the politics, religion, and culture of the period more fully than any other book.

Neale, John E. *Queen Elizabeth I.* London: J. Cape, 1959. This work illuminates the life of this Tudor queen in a novelistic style.

Pollock, John. *John Wesley*. Wheaton, Ill.: Harold Shaw, 1995. Skillfully written life of Wesley by Britain's foremost Christian biographer.

————. *Wilberforce*. New York: St. Martin's Press, 1977. This well-rounded, delightfully-written biography brings Wilberforce alive.

Reynolds, Barbara. *Dorothy L. Sayers: Her Life and Soul*. New York: St. Martin's Press, 1993. This work presents a well-rounded portrait of this extraordinary woman.

Roberts, Clayton, and David Roberts. *A History of England: Prehistory to 1714*. Third edition. New Jersey: Prentice Hall, 1991. Incorporates recent scholarship into a history of England that is broad in scope.

Sayer, George. *Jack: A Life of C. S. Lewis*. Second edition. Wheaton, Ill.: Crossway Books, 1994. It creatively details the life of C. S. Lewis's at the Kilns, his career at Magdalen College, and his relationship with Joy Davidman.

Scarisbrick, J. J. *Henry VIII*. Berkeley: University of California Press, 1968. A level-headed critical reassessment of Henry VIII.

Smith, L. B. *This Realm of England, 1399–1688*. Boston: Heath, 1966. This book insightfully recounts the interaction of the multiple factors that lead to the English Reformation and the final religious settlement achieved during the reign of Elizabeth and her Stuart cousins.

Stenton, Doris Mary. *English Society in the Early Middle Ages*. New York: Penguin, 1965. A charmingly-written account of English society with helpful chapters on towns, the church, and the arts.

Thomas, Keith. *Religion and the Decline of Magic*. New York: Scribner, 1971. Provides a useful treatment of pre-Reformation English popular religion.

Tuttle, Robert G., Jr. *John Wesley: His Life and Theology* (Grand Rapids: Zondervan). This title combines biography and autobiography in a helpful exploration of Wesley's theology.

Warren, Wilfred L. *Henry II*. Berkeley: University of California Press, 1973, eloquently presents a comprehensive, fair-minded reappraisal of the great Angevin king.

What to Read Before You Go

Let's Go: The Budget Guide to Britain and Ireland. New York: St. Martin's Press. Updated every summer by cost-conscious Harvard University students, this is the budget travelers' Bible.

Let's Go: London. New York: St. Martin's Press. This work provides the same conscientious service for the metropolis.

Steves, Rick. *Europe, Through the Back Door*. Santa Fe, New Mexico: John Muir Publications, 1995. This work is packed with valuable hints by this PBS travel guru with a keen sense of humor.

————. *Great Britain*. Santa Fe, New Mexico: John Muir Publications, 1996. Contains suggested trip itineraries with tips on avoiding tourist traps and scams.

What to Read While You Are There

Austin, Jane. *Persuasion*. New York: Penguin, 1994. A sparkling social comedy by this greatest of English women novelists. Explore England's western counties (Somerset, Dorset, Devon) in this and other novels by Austin (*Sense and Sensibility, Pride and Prejudice,* etc.).

Bronte, Emily. *Wuthering Heights*. New York: Cambridge University Press, 1997. One of the most haunting love stories in the English language, laid against the grim background of the windswept Yorkshire moors.

Chaucer, Geoffrey. *Canterbury Tales*. New York: Penguin, 1951. Remains one of the funniest and raciest stories in the English canon of literature.

Chesterton, G. K. *The Book of Father Brown*. Reprint, New York: Buccaneer Books, 1990. Follow this quirky, lovable cleric as he solves crimes with intuitive ingenuity.

Dickens, Charles. *David Copperfield*. New York: Signet, 1962. Delightfully details the trials, misfortunes, and adventures of youth in the countryside of Kent.

Doyle, Sir Arthur Conan. *Hound of the Baskervilles*. New York: Oxford University Press, 1993. Follow Sherlock Holmes and Dr. Watson across the English moor country.

Hardy, Thomas. *Tess of the d'Urbervilles*. New York: Cambridge University Press, 1996. Reveals the dark side of the Victorian Age on the fate-ridden Wessex landscape.

Herriot, James. *All Creatures Great and Small*. New York: St. Martin's Press, 1972. A heartwarming memoir of a Scottish veterinarian practicing his craft in the Yorkshire countryside.

Peters, Ellis. *A Morbid Taste for Bones*. Boston: Little and Brown, 1994. The first in a series of delightful suspense novels set in medieval Shrewsbury.

Sayers, Dorothy L. *Gaudy Night*. New York: HarperCollins, 1995. A suspenseful and terrifying tale that reveals to us the Oxford world of dons, students, and scouts.

————. *The Nine Tailors*. New York: HarperCollins, 1995. A classic murder story steeped in the parish atmosphere of the flat fen-country of East Anglia.

Stevenson, Robert Louis. *Dr. Jekyll and Mr. Hyde*. New York: Penguin, 1995. A fantasy thriller and moral allegory that immortalized old London's narrow, dark alleys and tall, huddled buildings.

Stoker, Bram. *Dracula*. New York: Oxford University Press, 1998. Opens with a visit to the mist-shrouded setting for Dracula's arrival in England at Whitby, Yorkshire.